SIMPLE PLEASURES

SHIRLEY PORTER

Simple Pleasures
Copyright © 2021 Shirley Porter

All rights reserved. No part of this publication may be reproduced or transmitted in any form or by any means without the written permission of the publisher. All rights reserved.

ISBN: 978-1-7358124-8-9

Contributing Editor: or all services completed
by Imprint Productions, Inc.
Cover Design: or all services completed
by Imprint Productions, Inc.

Printed in the United States of America
Published by Imprint Productions, Inc.
First Edition 2021

TABLE OF CONTENTS

CHAPTER I: THE SIMPLE PLEASURES	13
CHAPTER II: WHAT'S GOING ON?	16
CHAPTER III: IT'S MY PARTY TOO	19
CHAPTER IV: THE PLAN	22
CHAPTER V: THE BIG MISTAKE	26
CHAPTER VI: SUMMER FUN	29
CHAPTER VII: MARY JO AND THE GANGBUSTERS	32
CHAPTER VIII: THE TWIN'S HOUSE	36
CHAPTER IX: THE RED CLAY HILL CREEK	40
CHAPTER X: IT'S TOO COLD	43
CHAPTER XI: THE GREAT CHALLENGE	46
CHAPTER XII: THE BLACK HAWK CHERRY TREE	49
CHAPTER XIII: JOY THEN PAIN	52
CHAPTER XIV: SPILLING THE BEANS	55
CHAPTER XV: MAKING A POINT	58
CHAPTER XVI: WEEDING THE GARDEN	61
CHAPTER XVII: THE SUMMER RAIN	64
CHAPTER XVIII: WHY TODAY?	67

CHAPTER XIX: MARY JO'S MOMENT	70
CHAPTER XX: GIRLS ARE SPECIAL	73
CHAPTER XXI: THE GANG IS HERE	77
CHAPTER XXII: MAKING A PACT	79
CHAPTER XXIII: THE PEST, MR. SAM	82
CHAPTER XXIV: THE BIG BOX	85
CHAPTER XXV: RAIN, RAIN GO AWAY	88
CHAPTER XXVI: A SPECIAL TREAT	91
CHAPTER XXVII: THE BIG TOE AND A HARD ROCK	93
CHAPTER XXVIII: THE PAIN AND TREAT	97
CHAPTER XXIX: THE FACTS OF THE MATTER	101
CHAPTER XXX: A FRIEND INDEED	105
CHAPTER XXXI: THE PLAN	108
CHAPTER XXXII: THE ALLEY HUNT	111
CHAPTER XXXIII: DINNER FOR THE TWINS	113
CHAPTER XXXIV: CHASING A RAINBOW	118
CHAPTER XXXV: MAKING A QUILT	122
CHAPTER XXXVI: A SURPRISE VISIT FROM B.J.	124
CHAPTER XXXVII: THE PICNIC	129

DEDICATION

I would like to dedicate this book to my sister Norma, and my twin sister, Sandra. They are no longer with us, and I miss them dearly. Special thanks to my husband, Bernett Sr. for his support and my big sister Elizabeth, who is very much a part of this adventure and my oldest son Bernett Jr., he would constantly remind me to finish this book. My two children Deshonna and Levi who are also no longer with us, they both hold an extra special place in our hearts that especially helps me get through the hard times. The memories we shared were happy times and will last forever.

Shirley Porter

Simple Pleasures

PREFACE

An adventure does not have to be in a faraway place. It can happen right where you are. Children can use their creative abilities that lie just between their ears to find ways to explore and enjoy their environment through little things in nature and the natural world.

This book is for those who are young as well as those that are young at heart. It will bring back fond memories for those of us who remember the lazy days of summer when we played outside and found simple, creative ways to enjoy the day. It will encourage today's children to put away technical toys and gadgets for a bit, and begin the adventure of enjoying "The Simple Pleasures" and being a kid having lots of fun in the summertime.

Shirley Porter

Simple Pleasures

INTRODUCTION

Just inside of Tennessee's border is a small town that is so back in the boonies that folks say it fell off the map. Hardly anyone can find it. Johnson City is nestled like a baby in a valley surrounded by majestic mountains that seem to tower through the soft blue skies and the fluffy white clouds. A pictorial scene of beautiful rolling hills, fresh springs flowing down the mountainside, and a patchwork quilt of the farmland as far as the eyes can see.

Even before you come into the downtown area, you can hear the big fountain splashing in the middle of the square. The two old black wrought iron benches with planks for seats surround a tall pole wrapped in honeysuckle vines that fills the air with wild sweetness. Near the top of this pole, two flags...blowing in the wind. Adults come to get the entire town's latest gossip and little ears hear, go feed the pigeons that gather round for a free meal.

Across the street, red brick sidewalks will take you to the town's main stores like the Park-N-Belt store, Bob's drug store, Minnie's Boys and Girls shop, and Ken's shoe store. Further up Main Street is the fashionable district...This marks where only the rich people could afford to shop. Just around the corner is the Five and Dime where anyone could go. Next is Harvey's shoe shop, The Sears Catalog store, two theaters; one for the colored and white folks, and one for whites only. Ford's appliance store is a bit further down, followed by the Southern Pacific train station, two bus stations; the Greyhound and Trailway bus stations, and Bud's hamburger stand (the best burger your mouth ever tasted).

Dunbar Elementary, is a school built some forty years ago for the colored folks that sit on the other side of the tracks. For such an old school, it has an enormous amount of character; its weather-beaten red bricks on the outside showed no fear of the elements that have assaulted it over the years. The school building started at the corner of Elm Street and ends at the corner of Popular Street. Two large Elm trees sit on each side of the entrance, their leaves swaying lazily in the breeze.

Old-timers like Mr. Sam, Mr. Bob, old toothless Slim, and several others stop for a spell under the shade trees to play a game of checkers, or dominos but mostly reminisce about the years that have gone by. If you liked listening to the old stories, this was the place to be. Every now and then, Mr. Sam would pull out his handkerchief and with his hand, wipe the sweat from his brow while he slowly tells his tale. Toothless Slim responds with an Ah-hum or a Shore to everything said. Mr. Bob sits quietly on an Apple crate, fanning himself, chewing Beechnut Tobacco and reminding Slim, "it's your move, Ah-hum."

As the season changes from summer to fall, colored leaves put on a show, glittering in the morning dew. Mother Nature blows her frosty breath sending the leaves scurrying across the barren ground. Children's laughter would fill the air as they jumped and romped in the leaves piled as high as the sky.

Sometimes Mr. Bob and his dog Rover would sit on the old cobble steps just passing the time away. Mr. Bob watches the children play while Rover barks and tries to catch some leaves before they hit the ground.

Rover runs up the Cobble steps to the large doors with glass panes and faded wooden frames. His nose pressed against the glass, he can see the old screenless windows decorated with wild honeysuckle vines growing around their battered frames. Every now and then, you can taste the scent of the wildflowers. Flies and bees were about their business enjoying the sweet nectar that these flowers had to give.

In the back of the schoolyard is one big sliding board sitting in the shadow of the building. This would keep the sliding board from getting hot from the afternoon sun. Four swings held aloft with a large looping chain that suspended from big steel rods. The chains made a loud clanging sound as children swung as high as they could go. Cool wind whips across their faces, tears of joy fill their eyes and little voices sing, "Wee! Wee!" When recess was over, they paid "No, never mind" to the swings' wooden seats as they rubbed their splintered behinds.

On the other side of the schoolyard, boys played with a rounded stick and a rubber ball on the tightly packed red clay. You can hear them yell, "Hit that ball," as the batter would swing with all his might trying to imitate his favorite baseball player. His teammate would holler, "It's a home run," as the rubber ball soared up and out the yard.

They will be thinking about what lies ahead, so put away the books, pencils, and papers. It's time to think about the good times and rekindling of friendships. The silly songs, the quiet time, and the many games you will play. Winter has passed and summer is near where days are filled with delight as the fireflies dance in the night. So come along and get on board to fill your heart with a tale you might like. "Oh! The joy of being a kid in the summertime where your imagination runs wild to discover life's joy and a little pain. Just right outside your doors you find your dreams in the old and the good old summer time.

Simple Pleasures

CHAPTER I
THE SIMPLE PLEASURES

It was 2:30 p.m. on Friday June 2, 1944, at Dunbar Elementary School. The books were about to be closed and the end of another spring semester. Miss Hollingsworth, the third-grade teacher, was standing near the big open window trying to catch a breath of fresh air. At this time of the day, the weather tended to get warmer without a hint of breeze. The room was hot, and everyone felt sticky. However, this little class did not mind the extra discomfort they were feeling. The beautiful sound of the bell was about to ring and that would give them their freedom until fall.

Unexpectedly, Miss Hollingsworth said, in a very stern voice for "Everyone, remain seated after the dismissal bell rings."

The "Ah's," the "Hun's" and the "what for," roared through the classroom like a sound of thunder. The old woman, Miss Hollingsworth, was only twenty-three with smooth ebony skin, dark brown eyes that had the look of a tiger's eyes, and a slender frame that made her soft summer dress cling like the blue clematis on the mailboxes. She was a gentle woman, yet spoke with authority and she let the third-grade class know that she meant business.

Sitting in a state of shock, opened-mouthed and wide-eyed were thirteen pupils, seven boys and six girls. This class was overwhelmed, and astonished and quickly said, "This can't be, and this is not supposed to happen. It's summer and it's time to go." Exactly what was happening? No one had a clue.

Nevertheless, every class has its character and this class was no exception. Her name was Mary Jo Ruth Finney. She had a warped imagination but was the smartest in the class. She was One of those kids who were born before her time. This class would not have attempted to say what she said. Mary Jo, as she like to be called, played with her ponytail, as a thought ran through her mind. What should she do to get some answers? At that moment, she leaned forward, putting her elbows on the desk, and rested her chin in her hands. She thought I am not going to accept this. Then she decided to challenge Miss Hollingsworth.

Mary Jo said, as if to be clearing her throat, "Ah! Hum!" At that point, she raised her hand to get the teacher's attention.

Miss Hollingsworth said with a firm voice, "Yes! Mary Jo?"

"Ah! Rah!" Mary Jo said with a sassy attitude, "Uh, yes, teacher what am I going to tell my mama when I come home late this afternoon ma'am?" And really getting beside herself she said, "My mama ain't a dummy and she knows what time school is out."

By this time, the class was in a state of disbelief as they said, "Oh! No, she didn't." Miss Hollingsworth said as she kept her same quiet composure, "Perhaps, Mary Jo Ruth Finney, since you want to be the class clown and make everyone respond to your smart remarks, if some of your friends would like to join you, they can." She promptly walked across the floor again to stand in the doorway.

At that moment, a blanket of quietness hung over the room like a mass of fog. The atmosphere reeked of silence as it moved throughout the classroom. If an ant would have walked across the windowsill, you would have heard it. There among the restricted bliss, seated in the last row near the window, was Bill Ray. He was ten-years-old and the second oldest out of three brothers and one sister. His sister was two years older and in the seventh grade. He repeated the third grade twice and school was not that important. Billy Ray's desire was to fight in the war. He rarely paid attention to anything. But in an instant blurted out, "What did she say, huh, huh, huh?" "What did she say?" tapping Betty Louise on her shoulder.

Betty Louise, who is seated in front of him, was a shy, soft-spoken, skinny kid. She turns whispering, "Why don't you listen sometimes, Billy Ray and then you will know what the teacher said."

"OOOH! So, you not gonna tell me Betty Louise?" Billy Ray humorously asked as he continued daydreaming out the window and rubbing a scab on his elbow.

Betty Louise, politely explained to Billy Ray that the teacher wanted them to remain in their seats after the bell rings. Betty Louise, a little nervous and feeling anxious, quickly thought she is not telling this boy anything else. She turned back around and continued to sit quietly in her seat.

By this time, curiosity was like a plague in that room, and their little minds were all in overdrive. They were trying to figure out why Miss Hollingsworth was keeping them after school. It just did not make sense to them. This was the day of all days. The class will have their freedom for three months. No more homework, studying for a spelling test, learning those dreadful multiplications, or reading loud so the class can make fun of you. Discussing the matter did not seem to help this class, because their little minds could not come up with what was happening. Even the town doctors' identical twins, Shirley and Sandra, Sandy for short, got up enough nerve to raise their hands and see if their 'two cents worth' would get some answers. Nevertheless, this did not faze Miss Hollingsworth. She was always two-steps ahead of the twins the whole year. Miss Hollingsworth felt the need to let this class know, she was serious. The famous look, the eyes that all grown-ups used, now put into action.

    This class knew and was well aware and in tune with the "look." The room became silent and no one even attempted to speak or dared to move, or even look her way. All eyes systematically stared into space as if they were in a trance or pretended to see something interesting on the big, blank blackboard that took up most of the wall behind her desk. This class was looking for an answer to their question. Everything was now fruitless with no sense meaning to what was going on. What could the class do to find the answers?

    All at once, you could hear the sound of someone whining, like a baby that needed a dirty diaper changed. "I wanta go home," Barbara Ann said, but the class was in a still-of-the-night mode.

    They were very, very quiet as the whining sound echoed though out the room. This did not bother the teacher because she knew Barbara Ann acted like a baby all the time and did not give Barbara Ann what she wanted. She threw her head back and continued to stand in the doorway. You see Barbara Ann Parks' whining had always worked before. Her parents were old enough to be her grandparents, so to keep her quiet, they gave her whatever she wanted. Sandy, the motherly type, in the seat across from her, reached over and took Barbara Ann's little hand. Reassuring her, Sandy told her that Miss Hollingsworth had a big surprise for the class.

    Sitting on the other side of the twins was Mary Jo saying nonchalantly, "It is possible, but I doubt it. And if (as she pointed her finger) Miss Hollingsworth was going to give the class a surprise, we would have had it by now."

    Sandy, the spokesperson said, in a melodic tone of voice "Mary Jo, do you remember the chocolate raisins we gave you at lunch time?" "

    Ah hum!" She managed to hum, and not wanting to talk at this time.

    Mary Jo was getting a little bothered and aggravated. Sandy, with a big smile was telling a big one, "it's chocolate covered ants."

CHAPTER II
WHAT'S GOING ON?

Frustrated and angry, Mary Jo looked over at the twins and said, "Liar, liar, liar, you pee in the bed." She had a lot of spite in her eyes as she looked over and stuck out her tongue. She continued to annoy the twins by saying, "Ya, a, ya, ya, I do not care," and "Y'all know it ain't no surprise."

The twins did not want to get in any trouble by talking. They refused to answer this girl and not respond to her taunting. The twins did not want to get in trouble. At this point in time the twins decided that Mary Jo was not that important. They just wanted to go home, get out of their hot pin-a-fold dress and sit on the front porch drinking a cold glass of Kool-Aid.

This hot stuffy room was getting to everyone, and the children could not understand why they were just sitting there. You could hear, "What is going on? Every classroom that is down that hallway are out and about enjoying the summer."

It was a shame how Miss Hollingsworth would not tell the class what was going on. Maybe Mary Jo was not wrong after all. It leaves one to wonder if she is right for once. For a moment, Mary Jo's face seemed frozen in time. Then, as if a light came on in her little brain, she had it all figure out now. Miss Hollingsworth was going to get rid of the class one by one. Ah! That is why she is standing in the doorway with her arms folded, sour look on her face, and left foot tapping out a beat that would scare a dog. Yes! This is serious business, Mary Jo thought to herself. I know what's going on. Now I've got a plan, pointing at her nimble finger. At that moment, as if on a great stage getting to act out her part, she proudly decided to make a disguise. This is what I need now, as she gaily waved her arms. Boldly, getting out of her seat she looked around at her classmates and loudly proclaiming, "Time is a wasting." But her classmates did not seem to care; they just gave her an aggravating look.

During this time the teacher was not in the doorway but had stepped out into the hallway. A quick check of her senses, Mary Jo took her seat before the teacher returned to the doorway, she was in her own little world and nothing was going to stop her. Now is the opportune time she needed to put her plan together. Since the twins stopped talking to her, she could work on her disguise. Her nimble little fingers were busy tearing up a piece of paper from her tablet. She drew some eyes, a nose, and a mouth and poked the eyes, nose, and mouth out with her pencil. Exactly what she was going to do with the two rubber bands she took off her ponytails leaves one to imagine. Mary Jo realized that it would not be long before "they" would come for them.

Mary Jo, sliding down in her seat and spying out the place, felt safe with only two eyes peeping over her desktop. Shirley looked over at her but wasn't quite certain what she saw or what it meant. Having such an inquisitive mind she slowly said, "Mary Jo, why are you down in your seat like that huh? Why do you have that piece of paper on your face? To keep cool?"

"Huh!" Mary Jo said, "Such childish babble. I do not have time to…," as she paused as if to lose her thought. She quickly decided it is best not to answer the silly twins. Mary Jo continued to stare over her desktop eyeing the teacher.

Suddenly, out of the deep dark chambers of her mind, she emerged like a butterfly releasing itself from a cocoon. "Uh huh!" in a loud voice as she sprang up out of her seat. There, without a shadow of doubt, Mary Jo had forgotten where she was. She, entangled with her thoughts and so unaware of how loud the "Uh huh!" sounded.

For the most part, she still had her disguise on and figured Miss Hollingsworth could not tell who was behind the mask. The teacher, was not impressed by her reaction or how she looked.

In a disciplinary tone of voice she said, "Mary Jo Ruth Finney, you need to sit in the corner for five minutes. And before you come up here you better take that silly looking paper off of your face."
"Oh, yes ma'am," Mary Jo quietly said.

The whole class started giggling and slapping their desks. Miss Hollingsworth did not think it was that funny as she just looked at the class. The class immediately went into a mode of silence.

Mary Jo, very irritated and embarrassed, quickly walked toward the front of the room. She did not want to sit on that little stool over in the corner that's made for a little elf. "It's not for humans," she muttered.

She just knew that her rump was going to feel like a piece of lead when her five minutes were up. It seemed like hours had passed before Miss Hollingsworth told Mary Jo could return to her seat. She walked back to her desk rubbing her backside.

Another thought infiltrated and took over her little mind. One could only guess what her next move would be. With that warped mind of hers, she will keep one guessing.

Suddenly, the class stopped what they were doing. The sound of footsteps got closer as all eyes focused on the doorway. The empty, dimmed-lighted hallway echoed the voice of a man as Miss Hollingsworth stepped into the hallway again. This is all that Mary Jo wanted to hear.

She moved to the edge of her seat like a slithering snake. In a loud voice said, "Uh Huh, I knew they were coming to get us."

Miss Hollingsworth stepped back into the room and gave Mary Jo the 'look' to be quiet. After all, she was ahead of all these silly little classmates minus one B. J. She knew what was going to happen because her brain told her. She was feeling good about what had just crossed her thoughts. It was all coming together now, and the waiting is almost over. I will soon be out of this hot sticky room and out in the nice sunshine. I can see myself skipping alone by myself on the way home.

Simple Pleasures

CHAPTER III
IT'S MY PARTY TOO

Sandy was bored and decided to ask her classmates a question about coming to her party the next day. Her friend B. J. was a little whiz kid who wore horn-rimmed glasses and sat in the front row. He mostly stayed to himself except when he talked to Sandy.

It was hard for Sandy to get B. J.'s attention, "Pst, pst, pst, psssst B. J." He finally turned around, with his horn-rimmed glasses sliding down his nose saying in a very soft voice, "Yeah!" Actually, she did not want the teacher to hear her. "Would you like to come to my party tomorrow?" Sandy said.

She did not do a very good job of whispering because the teacher pointed her finger at Sandy and let her know this is her last warning. B. J. quickly turned around in his seat. He amused his self by continue playing with a ladybug he had found outside during lunchtime.

Sandy was fuming with a bad attitude, that her lips stuck out so far, a truck could have ran over them. She was so mad at Miss Hollingsworth that the veins in her neck looked as if they were about to pop. "How dare that teacher talk to me like that? I'm going to tell my daddy." Sandy decided to get back at Miss Hollingsworth through inaudible remarks.

All at once the class heard footsteps in the distance. The sound got closer as all eyes focused on the doorway. The empty, dimly lit hallway echoed the voice of a man as Miss Hollingsworth stepped into the hallway again. Again, Mary Jo moved to the edge of her seat like a slithering snake. She said in a loud voice "Uh Huh, I knew they were coming to get us." Miss Hollingsworth stepped back into the classroom and gave Mary Jo that look again to be quiet. This did not stop her from thinking out loud that she was smart and knew what was going to happen to the class. Feeling good about what she was thinking and did another one of her fiendish laughs.

The twins had completely forgotten about Mary Jo and were at each other's throats. Shirley was very peeved at Sandy as she looked over and wanted some answers.

Sandy knew that her sister was not too fond of that weird, horn-rimmed glasses wearing kid. She had the nerve to invite him to my party. "Huh?"

"I really do not like him." Shirley stuck her lips out and her eyes looked as big as two saucers. Sandy was on her sister like white on rice. She let her know it was both of theirs's party and not just her party. "It's my party too."

Shirley could not say anything else and in a very snobbish way made gestures with her hands. She really did not have a good reason for not liking B. J. except maybe, it's how he enjoyed playing with those old nasty bugs he loved. He does not even try to wash his hands either. Sandy was angry and let Shirley know she would invite everybody. She looked at Shirley and said "Pooh."

Sandy went on to make a point about Shirley's friend Billy Ray, whom she invited is so dumb. He could not find his way out of the third grade if they showed him the door. Sandy began to laugh at Billy Ray talking about being a pilot. "He does not know a wing from a propeller."

Miss Hollingsworth immediately put a stop to the girls' loud behavior. In a very stern voice she told the twins to take the front two seats, "this instant!"

"Oh! No, Uh! Yes, ma'am," the twins replied. They quickly walked up to the front. Sandy informed Shirley that she was going to tell their daddy.

For the most part, Shirley did not care one way or the other that her sister told their daddy. They took their seats and the teacher unexpectedly and gingerly patted them on their heads. The twins looked up and stared at the teacher in disbelief. They gave that poor woman a look as though they could have wrung her neck like a chicken.

Shirley leaned over and whispered to her twin, "that teacher has lost it. She has forgotten who daddy is."

Dr. Johnson was the only black physician in town and for those who loved in the surrounding areas, he delivered all of the twins' friends and even some of their parents. Miss Hollingsworth needed the good doctor a few weeks before. She knew that the twins had a good daddy, and that was a doctor. As the twins were sitting there, they felt the only thing to do now was to deal with the situation. They had plenty of time to think about their party tomorrow.

Mary Jo was not going to give up that easily. "Ah!" she said, and still wondered why all of a sudden Miss Hollingsworth would make such a fuss about the twins' talking. The whole class knows that this is all they do is talk and ask questions. Her suspicious little mind knew beyond a doubt that the teacher was getting ready to get rid of them. After all, Miss Hollingsworth was still standing in the doorway as if she was on guard duty. Mary Jo had heard her uncle Johnny tell her mother that he had to do guard duty one night so Mary Jo knew what it meant.

Then, out of curiosity, she glanced around the room, and noticed how no one seemed to be interested in what was about to happen to them. The children were just sitting idle, acting like a June bug on a watermelon rind waiting for their fate.

Proud Mary Jo thought, not me, with a wicked smile on her face. Her little deviant mind had a plan; she would ask the teacher when the class lined up if she may be excused, and I will make my escape out the side door. Her little conscience, the inner voice that speaks to you, started to bother her. What about your friends? Why not tell them your plans? Mary Jo arrogantly thinking, it is me and only for me. Anyway, I do not like these children. They are all spoiled brats. Unlike me, a sweet young girl. I am just too smart for this class, as she proudly sat back in her seat. Her little mind seemed to be rattling on and on. Actually, I am just as smart as the teacher is. These children are like the twins, they are all silly. Ah, I have better things to do than to be bothered with them. She was in one of her melodramatic moods again. There should be two of me like the twins. I am too smart to have all of this brightness for just little old me.

Several of the teachers told Mary Jo that she was a bright young person. She would have a good future. This brightness had infected the child's brains. Nothing now would change her plans. She was fixated on out-smarting whatever the teacher had planned for the class.

Now she was ready to put her plan into action. She sat waiting for the teacher to tell them to lineup. Deep inside, she felt good and knew that this was what she had to do. It was her idea that was going to get her out of the evil plot that the grown-ups were planning. Mary Jo put on her smart face with her eyes staring straight at the door. She tried hard not to blink her big brown eyes. However, it didn't work that way. She had her eyes like an eagle fixated on it's prey. Mary Jo refused to look around at her classmates. She knew that the clues to her plans was the teacher.

CHAPTER IV
THE PLAN

The mysterious person continues to walk fast down the hallway. Feeling restless, irritated and downright tired of the hot sticky room, Mary Jo went into deep thought. What could she do to get the teacher to excuse her? She put her hand up her chin trying to think of something that would work. This girl was like a mad scientist attempting to make their formula work.

"Oh!" She suddenly burst out saying, scaring her classmates. They all turned in their seats to see what was wrong with her. She gave the class a scornful look, feeling so proud of herself.

Every beat of her heart pulsated like the second hand on the big clock on the wall. Mary Jo felt good, as she continued to keep her eyes on Miss Hollingsworth. This plan she thought up was perfect. It definitely will work and would be free as a bird. She knew that time was on her side and any moment now her teacher would let her go.

Several of the boys were growing restless, hot, bored, and tried from just sitting in that room. To break the boredom and have little fun the boys had the audacity, except B. J., too start throwing spitballs when the teacher wasn't looking. The boy's main target was the girls who were sitting quietly in their seats. All at once, the spitballs were flying through the air like a missiles hitting their targets.

This fiendish act created quite a stir with the girls, all except for Mary Jo. On hearing all the commotion, Miss Hollingsworth stepped back in the room and let the class know that she hadn't dismissed them yet. In her stern voice of authority she said, "This is not the playground, keep quiet."

Once again, she turned and continued to talk to someone in the hallway. This was not what the class wanted to hear, the teacher reminding them that they were not on the playground. Murmured voices could be heard because the class could not understand or make out what was being said. In that moment, heavy footsteps could be heard running back down the hallway.

Simple Pleasures

Miss Hollingsworth returned to her post in the doorway wishing they would hurry up. Thinking this is too long to keep the children in this hot sticky room. She could feel the heat in the room getting to her too. She knew the fever of summer was getting into her blood too like the children. She laughed and continued to look down the hallway keeping an eye on her pupils.

Mary Jo took the opportunity and seized the moment to raise her little hand and said, "May I be excused please?"

Miss Hollingsworth, realizing that the children had been in the room for a while said, "Mary Jo, we all will be going in a few minutes and then you may be excused." Perhaps Mary Jo's plan was working. All she had to do now was to wait in the bathroom until the class outside.

Miss Hollingsworth's patience was wearing definitely thin as time seemed to stand still. She decided that this was enough and immediately, had the class to stand, and form one line, and continually walking out to the playground. Would you just know it, Miss Mary Jo decided that she would go to back of the line.

This was not Miss Hollingsworth's plan. The teacher told the twins in a very sweet tone of voice, go to the back of the line. Sandy and Shirley shrugged their shoulders and looked at Miss Hollingsworth with eyes that were throwing daggers.

While Mary Jo was in her own little world, thought, huh, my plans are spoiled again. She decided that this would be even better because she would be third from the last. She would not have to wait that long to leave. "Hot Dog!" She mumbled, I'm the best."

The children continued to line up without paying any attention to this half-crazed girl. They were all too happy to be leaving the hot classroom. The children all gaily walked down the dimly lit hallway and as they approach the girl's bathroom, Miss Hollingsworth motioned for Mary Jo to step out of line to be excused.

Mary Jo felt a moment of triumph and glory as she headed for the bathroom. A song of joy was ringing out from her and throughout the empty bathroom. "I'm free, free, free, I'm getting out of here. I'll just wait until I hear everyone on the playground."

While standing there she thought, I better go ahead and use the bathroom since I'm in here. Does not make too much sense to wait until I get home. Huh, I might not make it, as she laughed at what she was thinking. While sitting there taking care of her business she could hear a ramming noise. It was a motor. "Uh hum! Yes, yes, it was a truck I heard and they are loading them up now. Oh! Thank you, thank you for letting me be so smart."

For a moment, Mary Jo looked confused and puzzled at what she was hearing, she couldn't believe it. The children were cheering and singing "Happy Birthday" to the twins. Still trying to convince herself that this was not, could not be, what her litter ears was hearing.

Mary Jo quickly told her heart to be still. She wanted to hear what was going on outside. She tried holding her breath so she could hear; however, her heart was beating louder because of the anxiety she was feeling. The sound of her heartbeat began to sound very loud in her ears. Those little ears of hers were not playing a game on her. The children were really singing "Happy Birthday" to the twins.

"What is this?" While trying to understand the reason the children were singing "Happy Birthday" today. She definitely heard the twins inviting the children to come to their party tomorrow. She hurriedly got though with her business. By this time, Mary Jo was still a little confused trying to figure out what was happening outside. She quickly and nervously washed her hands, and like a flash of light, she ran over to the bench under the window.

Mary Jo tried to look out, but she was too short. Actually, the bench was like a little cot for the fourth, fifth and sixth-grade girls to use during "those times." She had to stand on her tiptoes and hold onto the windowsill to see out. What she saw on the playground shocked and amazed her. There were clowns, balloons, party hats, streamers, hot dogs, sodas, popcorn, a big birthday cake, and someone's mother was making homemade ice cream. Children were laughing and having fun, and were taking turns riding the two ponies that the twins had received for their birthday.

By now, poor little Mary Jo was so overwhelmed that she sat down on the cot and began to cry. As tears ran down her little face, she realized that the teacher did have a big surprise for the class after all. "Oh!!! No wonder the children did not pay any attention to me. The class had to know that the twins were having their party today."

CHAPTER V
THE BIG MISTAKES

While the kids celebrated, Miss Hollingsworth began to wonder what was taking Mary Jo so long? She has been in the bathroom for quite a while now. The teacher began to think, maybe she should check on her. As she walked across the playground, she felt her heart fill with joy. This was truly the best surprise she had seen in years.

The children were surprised, and the twins' parents really know how to give a party. A tear stained her eyes as she began to remember this class was truly a handful. Especially the darling little twins asking so many questions all of the time. She smiled thinking about the different children that crossed her mind at that moment.

On the playground, the children were having the time of their lives. There were happy faces everywhere. The twins were enjoying riding their ponies. Other children were playing "pin the tail on the donkey," "spin the bottle," guessing how many jelly beans were in the big mason jar and jumping rope. Joyful sounds from the children who were patiently waiting for a clown to paint their faces.

The smartest girl in her class was missing the twin's birthday. That brightness she so proudly worked for and was used in the wrong way. The whole class is outside where a cool breeze is blowing, playing games, riding the ponies, and getting their faces painted.

"What happen?" Everything was pointing to Miss Hollingsworth and that mystery man who was walking fast up and down the dim-lit hallway. They were acting suspicious with the teacher stepping out in the hallway. The class could hear only the two of them whispering and they were still left clueless. On the other hand, Mary Jo knew that she had the answer and outsmarted all her classmate. How did she get her clues so wrong as she sat there with her head down and the tears lapping under her chin.

What a foolish plan she has come up with. There on the playground was the surprise of all times. The classmates she felt was silly child are outside wearing party hats, blowing the toy horns and playing with the many balloons. How bad Mary Jo was feeling as the tears flowed down her little face as if it was raining. The thought crossed her mind was none of the kids missed her. They were having too much fun to realize she was not outside.

Miss Hollingsworth walked across the playground, looking at the children enjoying the party and having fun. This party was definitely worth the time, the poor little darlings had to sit in that hot sticky room. The noise the children were making, mostly the girls, were kind of bothersome. Mary Jo and the twins had gotten under her skin too, but it was all right now.

Nearing the bathroom, she wondered did Mary Jo decide to go home. Anyway she decided first to check the bathroom too made sure. Miss Hollingsworth thought she heard someone sobbing. Quickly, open the door she hurried in and sitting on the little cot, was Mary Jo.

"My, my, my, why all the tears? How come you are not outside with the rest of the children? Are you sick? Is it the big thing happening ? What is the matter Mary Jo?"

Miss Hollingsworth paused as she found herself asking one question after another. Poor child did not have time to catch her breath. Between the sobbing, she could not answer the questions. Then the teacher said, "Mary Jo, I haven't given you a chance to answer any of my questions, huh?"

This was so overwhelming as Mary Jo tried to get her composer back and through the tears she said, "It is really a party for the twins?" There was really a surprise for us.

"Yes!" Mary Jo, Miss Hollingsworth gaily said. "It's the twins' birthday party today. Their parents wanted all their classmates to enjoy the last day of school with a big party. Now dry your eyes and wash your face," Miss Hollingsworth said. "There's a party outside waiting for you to come to."

Mary Jo was off that little cot like a flash of lightening. She quickly washed her tear-stained face and out of the bathroom door, she ran. As she passed Miss Hollingsworth, she had as big smile on her face. Miss Hollingsworth chuckled as she went out behind her.

Things begin to look great now for Mary Jo who thought she had the answer. Her imagination went too far, and she almost missed the big party. All is well now and her eyes saw the big things that were happening out on the playground.

Her eyes could not believe all the things the children were doing. She thought, enough wasted time on my selective behavior. This is the party of all parties playing out on the playground.

Mary Jo threw up her hands saying, "Wow, golly gee! What a surprise!" She went over to where the twins were playing and joined in. She rode the pony acting like the cowboys that Billy Ray enjoyed watching at the movies. B. J. was playing spin the bottle, while the twins tried to guess how many jellybeans were in the big Mason jar? Everything was good now, as the class played and ate until they all shouted "No More!"

Billy Ray, B. J., the twins and even whinny Barbara had a ball with Mary Jo. That day at the party, the kids found out that they really liked each other. While walking home that evening the little group formed a bond. They decided as they talked, laughed, and played together, their friendship should continue.

Billy Ray said, "This party was better than the fireworks at the Fourth of July County Fair." He looked over at B. J. wanting him to respond.

B. J. was all smiles when he said, "You bet, Billy Ray." Even Mary Jo seemed to finally come to her senses. Thinking she knew this was the best time of her life today. Whinny Barbara could not remember when she had this much fun. Today broke the record for fun. The twin's party topped everything that the group had experienced. Especially for Barbara, this definitely was a high time for her. She rarely got the chance to play with other children. Most of her time was with her older parents. This was without a doubt what the poor child needed, to play with other children. Her eyes lit up as she finally experienced what a joy just playing with children her age. The children held hands and let out a yell. This was for the good time they had today. Now, truly this was going to be the best summer ever. They marked the twins party as the first day of summer fun.

Mary Jo suggested, since they were going to hang out together during the summer that they need a plan. Her little mind was working and came up with the second thing they could do.

B. J. did not give her time to share with them before he shouted, "Oh! Boy!" Mary Jo did not mind the interruption as she told her new friends that she would share with them later. She would sleep on it and would let them know later on.

Simple Pleasures

CHAPTER VI
SUMMER FUN

Having the time of their lives, Mary Jo could now use her imagination on happy times. She decided that everyone should meet at her house tomorrow and they could talk about it. The crew were going to have a lot of fun. "Yeah!!" they all yelled, "That's a good idea Mary Jo. You are so smart," Billy Ray abruptly replied, looking strange. For some reason Mary Jo accepted his regards without any fanfare. Billy Ray was a happy boy now that he finally passed. He had some new friends that did not pay that much attention to him before. Life for Billy Ray seemed to change for him because of the party. Now he had something to look forward to in the fall going to the fourth grade.

B.J. sounded as if it was so hard for him to pass to the fourth grade. Hum! B. J. thought, I am the smartest one in the class besides Mary Jo. He did a little chuckle with a smile on his face.

The girls, on the other hand, did not say anything about passing. They already knew how hard it was for Billy Ray to finally get out of the third grade. The brainy B. J. was not even worth discussing. He was really the brain of all brains.

Clearing his throat B. J. said, "Hey, Billy Ray, maybe we can look at some books about airplanes while we are out, ok?"

Feeling a little anxious and surprised, he nodded and was happy that B. J. invited him. B.J. did read a lot and most likely there were some books in his room on planes. He knew how much Billy Ray enjoyed looking and talking about planes. Especially, when he was in class and would hear a plane flying over.

Billy Ray's pastime in class was being non-attentive but listen and look out of the windows. This boy would sit, biting on his nails, making humming sounds and hoping to hear or see an airplane pass over. B. J. wanted to help and let him enjoy finding out what he was interested in.

Even though, B. J. was the scientist that enjoyed bugs, birds, butterflies, and critters of all kinds. The weirder the critter, the better B.J. liked them. He decided he was going to help Billy Ray find about all kinds of planes.

Mary Jo did not need to explain herself, she was the planner who enjoyed others praising her. She enjoyed getting things done and the feeling of being in charge. Everyone was happy now as she looked over and asked Barbara what was she doing over the summer Mary Jo really did not want to know, but asked Barbara that question so she would not feel left out.

Barbara was glad to be a part of the group, even if for a little while. She happily said in her whining voice, "My daddy and mama and me are going upstate New York to see some kinfolks that I've never met. We'll be leaving on Sunday at 4 p.m. on the train."

Billy Ray, being intrusively, said. "Boy! That is something I always wanted to do, ride on a train."

"Me too, Billy Ray, this could be something special huh, the gang riding on the train." B. J. abruptly said. Left up in the air about the train ride, they continued discussing other things, they could do for the summer. Everything the boys suggested doing, the girls acted silly jumping up and down and laughing.

Dropping off Barbara at home, Mary Jo was still enjoying the pleasures of summer and said joyfully, "How happy all of us are today."

"Yeah!" One could hear all of them say. Mary Jo was so happy.

B. J., looking up at the sky as the twilight of the evening was breaking through, with poetic thought expressed himself, "This summer is going to be the simple things we are going to do and getting the pleasures out of doing them."

The gang was wide-eyed with disbelief, as they stared at B. J. and what he just spoke. A big, "Wow!" as the gang continued to stare at B.J.

Mary Jo could not help but look at this boy and the statement he made. He is smarter than I thought he was. A little genius on our hands, Mary Jo continued to think. No wonder he sat at the head of the class. She laughed in silence and waved good-bye to her friends as she headed for her house.

It was like being in a fairy tale from all the fun things that had happened at the party. The fun things the twins' parents planned for all of us were outstanding. Mary Jo was happy that things did not turn out like she imagined in that weird mind of hers as she walked down the path to her house.

Enjoying the moment, she reflected back on the silly things that happened that day. It was exciting, hot, sticky, and most of all, the mystery part of the day, the surprise party. Hitting her forehead with the palm of her hand she would never let her imagination go that deep in the shadows of her mind again.

However, earlier in the week Mrs. Johnson shared with Mrs. Hollingsworth about giving the twins a birthday party the last day of school. Mary Jo is going to be shocked when she finds out that her mama did not tell her. Knowing her mama, she will tenderly sit her down at the table and tell her the story.

Mary Jo was tired and all she wanted to do now was climb in her mama's big bed and sleep. The day had been one of the best yet but her little body had enough. She hastened her step as she hurried home to sharing with her mama the ball she had at the party. Mary Jo smiled and thought, "My mama is not going to believe the wonderful party we had today. It was better than the Fourth of July picnic."

Nothing could beat the wonderful times they spent at the picnics, until now, this party was the best. The boys got to know the girls and how much fun they could have playing together. The excitement rose up in Mary Jo as she could see her house. She began to run as fast as her feet could take her. Hurrying up the steps and out of breath she paused just to catch her breath.

CHAPTER VII
MARY JO AND THE GANGBUSTERS

Now that summer was about to begin, Mary Jo's thoughts were on how much fun they were going to have. She decided first the gang could go down to Bay Creek and dam it up. Then they would be able to go for a nice cool swim, just to feel that cool water hastened at her footsteps. She headed to B. J.'s house, about four blocks from her house.

Mary Jo chose to walk in the middle of the road instead of the path. She really did not like the thought of all those critters that crawled around in the tall grass, nor those big black and yellow bumblebees and wasps that are attracted to the beautiful wildflowers.

Thinking out loud, as if to let the critters and snakes know that she was not walking near the path. "Who knows," with a troubled look on her face, as Mary Jo pondered, how many snakes are in that grass? Just in case there might be some snakes, they will not have to worry about my coming over there disturbing them.

Quickly hasting her steps, Mary Jo decided continued on the road. When a car comes, I'll just move to the side of the road, she thought. Feeling brave Mary Jo said, "How many people in this town own a car? Two people at the most," as she chuckled to herself, and continued skipping down the road. She was doing the right thing, the road was the best and safest place for Mary Jo to walk, those weeds did have poison ivy just waiting to get on somebody's skin.

The fear of snakes was a good thing because there were snakes over in the tall grass. Actually, there were garter snakes, lizards and a few field mice.

B. J. on the other hand was not afraid of any reptiles, wild animals or creepy, crawling critters. This kid was born with the instinct for finding and treasuring them. He loved the outdoors and found some interesting things in those woods behind Mary Jo's big, old two-story house that he would bring home. All the kids that came over to his house said, "His room looked like a mad scientist's laboratory."

Finally, getting to B. J.'s house and standing in the front yard, Mary Jo yelled out his name several times making sure he heard her. Looking out his window he shouted, "I will be out in a minute." She had to shade her eyes with her hand. But decided not to response with words but motion with her hand for him to come on down.

While standing there she could feel the heat of the morning and knew this was going to be a great day. She did not want to waste too much time as B. J. promptly came running out the door.

B. J., looking at Mary Jo was smiling and so glad to see her. He was still happy from the great birthday party the twins had. Mary Jo, being very reserved, let B. J. have his say without interrupting him. He was so overjoyed at the good time they had that day.

Mary Jo did not want B. J. to keep asking her questions while she told him of her plans for the summer. She noticed how excited and happy this boy was. One would have thought the twins' party was his. Poor thing, he did not have any sisters or brothers to play with either. Mary Jo just nodded her head as B. J. went over the same things she already knew.

Finally, B. J. got around to asking, "What are the plans for today?" She hesitated, but did not respond but walked away very fast. B. J. almost had to run to keep up with her little feet. He was huffing and puffing as if he was running a race. She stopped and said, while trying to sound impressive and acting like it was a big secret, "I'll talk about it when we go and get the others."

B. J. was surprised at her not telling him and gave her a weird look. Even though it was just a half mile to Billy Ray's house, it felt as if they had been walking for hours. The sunny hot days in June were sometimes unbearable. The air was so thick you could almost cut it with a knife. Whatever breeze would come up was only lazily rippling. You would only notice the breeze by the trees and the tall grass swaying. It was so hot that at times you could see the heat waves rising up off the ground and the pavement looking like steam coming out of it. Going barefoot and even walking on the dusty powdery road did not make it any better.

For the most part, Mary Jo could go without a top. She still had mosquito bumps on her chest and it did not matter whether she had a shirt on or not. Being a little concerned, B. J. abruptly questioned Mary Jo about her sandals. Instead of her answering B. J. she had to go into one of her routines again. She was rocking from side to side just popping her lips, with a long drawn out sound, "Well-ll-ll! I was thinking, I would not need then."

Mary Jo was not born yesterday, B. J. thought. Every month during the summer, the weather is hot, humid and it rains mostly every day. How dare her to think the weather would be any different than today. Mary Jo sensed that B. J. did not go along with her answer because he did not say anything else.

She wanted him to know that she was in a hurry to get the gang. The weather felt good this morning but she got fooled. Now, "Shoo! It's hot enough to cook a marshmallow on this road, huh B. J."

B. J. did not answer but knew her feet felt the heat. Anyway, B. J. knew that they would pass right by her house and could get her sandals then. Without responding to Mary Jo, B. J. continued to walk toward Billy Ray's house.

It did not take them long once they started walking a little faster. They quickly came up to Billy Ray's front gate. During, this time, the wonder boy scientist, B. J. spotted a moth butterfly. His eyes lit up like a kid opening his presents on Christmas day. He was running around shouting, "Gee whiz! I have struck it rich. This is what I have been looking for! Wow! Golly! Gee!"

Mary Jo made a face and did not say anything. She was thinking, of course, as she put her hand on her forehead. That's all I need in my life now is to have nature boy spot a rattle snake. In her melodramatic way, she put on an act that could have gotten her a role in a movie. "Oh! Why? Why? Why? Why do I put up with this silliness?"

It did not faze or bother B. J. He glanced her way and continued trying to catch his prize. While all this drama was going on between Mary Jo and B. J., Billy Ray was on the side of the house. He noticed Mary Jo coming through the gate looking displeased.

"Hi, Mary Jo, how have you been?" Billy Ray said.
Mary Jo motioned for B. J. to come on. He quickly stopped chasing butterflies and let out a big "Wee!" sound.

More drama was about to unfold before Mary Jo's eyes. Billy Ray, looking up in the sky spotted his dream and shouted, "Will you look at that beauty? That's a DC-10 passenger plane," acting more excited. "Mary Jo I bet'u ah, that they have troops on it too."

As the old folks say, "This beat all," in other words nothing can top what this boy is seeing right now. Mary Jo stood in disbelief as she stared at this boy getting excited over an ugly airplane. She put her hands on those bony hips and let out a big sigh.

In the meantime, Billy Ray had his arms stretched out waving back and forth making those sounds like an airplane, "vroom, vroom, vroom, vroom." He defiantly was creating and making a nuisance out of himself. Pausing for a second and trying to figure this out, Mary Jo decided she was just wasting her time. A loud "No-o-o-e!" sound came out of her being.

This immediately got Billy Ray's attention as he acted as if he were a little kid glancing over at Mary Jo staring at him. He stopped making the noise and slyly smiled and started walking down the road. Mary Jo and B. J. did not say anything but had to hurry to catch up with him. It did not take long to get back to Mary Jo's house. It seemed like getting the boys took her longer than she thought. She anxiously called out to her mama, as she ran through the house. Her mama, coming from the kitchen wanting to know "what was all the shouting about?"

"Where are my sandals mama?" Mary Jo asked.

Her mama smiled and pointed to the upstairs and Mary Jo knew what it meant when her mama gave her the silent treatment. Go look where shoes are supposed to be. Mary Jo humbly hung her head and ran up the stairs to bedroom. She went straight to the closet and rummaging through her mama's closet. She found her sandals and put them on. Mary Jo waved goodbye to her mama and out the door she went.

CHAPTER VIII
THE TWIN'S HOUSE

The sun was becoming unbearable as the gang walked down the hill to get to the twins' house. The twins lived in a big white house built between two big maple trees. This house had a look of elegance and warmth that surrounded the space it occupied. There were white picket fences around the property and up the walk. On both sides were colorful flowers. Two big red and white rose bushes were on each side of the front near the porch.

The porch wrapped around on both sides of the house. On the left side of the porch was a swing and some chairs. The right side was screened and had a white wicker set where the family sometimes ate during the hot summer. Large flowerpots graced each side of the big door. Actually, their house was the best-looking house around.

B. J., Billy Ray, and Mary Jo walked up the steps to the huge door and rang the doorbell. The maid looked out the window on the door and saw some little people on a mission. She slowly opened the door and asked, "May I help you?"

Mary Jo said, "I would like to see the twins please."

The housekeeper said, "Shirley and Sandy are playing on their swings in the backyard. Yawl go around the house that way," and pointed to the right side of the house.

Mary Jo, B. J., and Billy Ray walked down the steps and went around the house. This really peeved Mary Jo. You could see her expression changing and a sour look was on her face. She felt that the housekeeper could have told the twins we were here. So irritated she said aloud, "Isn't that what a maid does?"

Wouldn't you just know it, they could hear the maid talking from the back door telling the twins that there were some kids who wanted to see them. Mary Jo rushed around the house to give this old maid a piece of her mind. However, that thought changed when she saw the twins running over to greet them. In a squeaky voice the twins said, "Mary Jo, B. J., Billy Ray, it's so nice to see you all again." It seemed they

Simple Pleasures

had a thousand questions to ask. "How has it been? What's up for the summer? What have you guys been doing since the party?"

"Whoa! Hold up on the questions, just one-minute twins," Mary Jo said."

Speaking for the rest of the gang, Mary Jo let the twins know that they were doing all right. "We cannot thank you two enough for the good time at your party." The twins were overjoyed to see the kids come by. Now it's time to have some fun. They have not had any fun since the party. Their mom and dad went on a vacation and really have not been out of the yard at all.

Sandy said, with her mouth poked out, "That old maid Mabel, told us that our mama said to not let us out of the yard."
"Yeah," Shirley followed, as she told her side of what was going on. She made her point by telling Mary Jo, Billy Ray, and B. J. the time Mabel put them to bed at 7:30p.m. At that time of day, the sun is still light. It is summertime and it is time to have some fun. The twins went on to tell the little group how miserable they were. They needed to be recused from the dull summer. And to add to their problems, Mable was acting as if she is somebody's mama, as Shirley looked for a response from Sandy.

Sandy exclaimed as she added to the problem they were experiencing with Mabel. The twins needed to be free from their boring backyard and it definitely needed to be today. Now that the gang let the twins have their say, the gang was excited about getting ready for the summer.

Mary Jo quickly let the twins know that the gang is going to have a lot of fun. This really made the twins feel bad. They knew "old rubber butt" Mable whom the twins called when they are mad at her, was not going to let them go anywhere. This little gang needed to come up with a quick idea to get the twins out of their yard.

Shirley had a plan but was somewhat doubtful if it would work. They decided that they try to use it anyway. Knowing that was Mr. Henry, sitting at their table last night, the twins would ask Mabel if that was Mr. Henry they saw last night sitting at the table eating our food. This sounded like a good plan, but the kids knew the rule: "Kids are to be seen and not heard." This did not put a damper on their plan. They knew the rule for grown-ups too. Mabel was not to let anyone in the house until the twins' parents return home. They knew they had the upper hand on Mabel now because she broken a rule. This was a time to be elated as they put their plan in action. They all let out a big cheer.

The twins ran up the back porch steps into the house. "Mabel, hey, Mabel,

Mabel," the twins cried out. Mable did not seem too concerned with the twins calling her and continued fixing the table.

Slowly turning around asking, "What do yoes won't?"

During this time, they were somewhat afraid to ask Mable. Shirley looked at Mable and said, "Can, can we go with the kids for a while? We won't stay long. Can we, can we," the twins asked.

Sandy was a very wise girl. She seized the moment and asked Mabel, "Ah, uh, uh, ah was that Mr. Henry sitting at the table last night?"

Mabel began to fuss with the tablecloth and cordially said, "Can't ya see I'm cleaning? I got to git through here so as I can fix yawl supper. Now just git on out of my way now. Y'all make shore ya all don't stay out there too long, ya heah?"

Sandy and Shirley were happy and said they would be back around four o'clock. Mabel nodded her head then pointed to the four on the clock that hung on the kitchen wall. She did not need to say too much to the twins. They could read Mable's silent remarks and knew what she meant without her saying anything.

The twins said at the same time again, "Okay," and in an instant they were out the door. Mabel shouted, "Look out here comes the gang busted." She laughed, waved her hand goodbye and went back in the house to prepare their supper.

Mabel was just like a second mother to those girls. She was there when they were born. She really was good to those twins taking care of them, and she knew they were crazy about her, too. Mabel was just keeping the twins until their parents returned from their vacation, otherwise, Mabel just worked three days for the family.

CHAPTER IX
THE RED CLAY HILL CREEK

The happy sound of children laughter could be heard as they head down the street. Wow! Oh golly!" The twins busted out happily saying. The little gang could not hardly wait to get to Red Clay Hill Creek. The twins enjoy splashing around in the water and blowing bubbles with their mouths.

B. J. totally agreed with what the twins were saying. He was ready to swim and splash around in the water, too. He had plans for the twins and their big challenges. He did not realize that the twins could indeed swim now. Their parents gave them swimming lessons when they would go on vacations. They learned how to hold their breath and kick their feet under the water.

 In the meantime, Mary Jo felt the gang was wasting too much time. She solemnly said, "It's already 12:30 and we still have other things to do today. I like going swimming, but there is something special I would like for us to do today."

Immediately, they all stopped as if they were frozen in time as they wondered what was the special thing Mary Jo had planned? Billy Ray, overexcited did not give Mary Jo a chance to answer. He wanted to know right then and there what it was. The twins and B. J, just stared at her waiting for her to tell them.

Mary Jo did not respond. She gave Billy Ray one of her great stares as she tapped her foot in disbelief. The tension was mounting as the little gang stood around her staring with their mouths open. The twins' eyes were sparkling in the sunlight as the suspense mounted.

Mary Jo was like one of those characters right out of the comic books and movies. The stuff she would come up with when she was in her creative mode was so believable. Her well-kept secret at last was going to be revealed as she slowly popped her lips. "This is the time of year when the fruit trees are ready for the picking." The focused deviant mind of Mary Jo was on Mr. Henry's black hawk cherry tree.

Intensifying, the little gang's imagination she painted a picture for their little minds.

"They are begging us to come and get them. Can't you just see them shining in the sun light, just waiting to be picked?" The built-up excitement hit that little gang like a firecracker making their little brains exploded with the sweet, black, round juicy cherries in their mouths.

Quickly thinking about what Mary Jo had just said, B. J. begin to wonder and doubt, "Are the cherries ripe now?"

Being dumbfounded and frustrated, Mary Jo ground her teeth and hit her hands. She knew that brainy B. J. was about to ask her a dumb question. Before he could say anything, she was all up in his face. B. J.'s eyes were glaring, and he could feel her hot breath all in his face. Mary Jo did not get the chance to sound off on B. J. He did a move that you would only see Flash Gordon do. He left Mary Jo standing there, looking silly and wondering, what happened.

Mary Jo looked around and noticed the little gang walking down the road. She got herself together swiftly walking and caught up with them.

Never once did it occur to the gang about asking Mr. Henry. That would be the right thing to do, ask if they could have some of his cherries? Neither did they think of the consequence that they might have to face. All they could think about right then was having fun and enjoying themselves. Billy Ray was not making too much sense, decided that he would say one of those figures of speech. "Mr. Henry shore sweet to Mabel. Don't you think so Mary Jo?"

Billy Ray was not smart on the saying that the older people would say. Aside from being smart, Mary Jo with her nosy self, did not leave any stone unturned. She would have her ears in hearing distant to overhear what older people were talking about. She figured out who or what they were saying.
Nevertheless, she nonchalantly explained with her smart-acting self to Billy Ray, that if he was going to say something say it right. Popping her lips, moving from side to side and waving her hand said," It's Mr. Henry is sweet on Mabel, okay?"

Billy Ray nodding his head and looking at Mary Jo with a questionable look in his eyes agreed. In front of the gang was Red Clay Hill. The gang thought about how much fun they were going to have. This place is where you start at the top of the hill and roll all the way to the bottom. The big mounds of dirt are a great place to hide behind. They could act like the cowboys, or play out the many war movies that they had the pleasure of seeing.

On the other hand, the twins were so glad to be out of the yard now. They ran around each mound yelling to the top of their lungs. They were acting as if they have never been out of their yard and did not care. This is what children should be doing, playing in the dirt, making loud noises, and discovering new things to do. The twins enjoyed chasing each other and climbing up the clay hill. They did not care about getting their nice, starched shorts and shirt dirty playing in the red clay.

In the meantime, Mary Jo and B. J. decided to hide in the mounds and dig in the red clay looking for lost treasures. Sometime the older kid like to come and ride down the hill on a piece of cardboard. Before they would get to the bottom of the hill, they would fall off and drop their change. Then they would pretend they were in the Army fighting in the war. They would be acting out what they saw at the movies. The older boys would shoot at each other with sticks and fall rolling down the hill.

This hill was a grand place to play and use your imagination. The children could create and pretend whatever they wanted to be. Billy Ray was too excited to hang around the hill with the gang. He was ready to go swimming. He left the rest of the gang to go on ahead and dam up the water. They all agreed and continued to play on the hill. Everything was going as planned except asking Mr. Henry if they could have some of his cherries. This did not cross their minds as they were enjoying one of the simple pleasures of summer, and did not think about the consequences. Who cared anyway, its summer and time to let go and have some fun.

Simple Pleasures

CHAPTER X
IT'S TOO COLD

On getting to the creek, Billy Ray was surprised; someone had already dammed up the water. It was all ready for five kids to enjoy. Immediately, he jumped in the cold water for a swim. He swam by himself until the gang decided to come. B. J. was the first to try it out as he ran and leaped into the water. As he came up for some air he noticed that the girls had finally made it. He waved his hand yelling for them to come on in. He splashed and dived, waiting for the twins and Mary Jo to join in. Billy Ray was enjoying himself as he climbed up on the bank. He was feeling the warm sun heating up his cool body. This was what he needed right then. But too much sun would make it hard to get back into the water. His body would warm back up to its normal temperature, so he would have to get his body use to the cold water again.

There is a big tree the boys just love to swing from. Billy Ray ran to the big tree grabbing the rope and swung himself out over the water. He made a big splash as he hit the water hard. He felt the sting on his body. That definitely was a belly flop and it hurt too bad to rub his belly. All he could do was moan.

The twins and B. J. teased Billy Ray about his great belly flop. He did not pay them 'no never mind' as he swam under the water. Mary Jo decided that she would take her time and wade in the cold water. Definitely, this would take longer for her to get use to the water. She shivered and pulled her feet out of the water. She jumped back on the bank as if some unknown creature was nibbling at her toes.

She decided that the water was just too cold. Her little body was turning blue. "This water is cold," as she convinced herself to get out. She waited for a response no one said anything. It was time for her to go into her melodramatic act again saying, "Oh! No-ooo-oo-oo!" Quickly she wrapped her arms around herself and shivered. Looking at the goose bumps on her arm really caused her to perform. She wanted the gang to look at her turning blue and the goose bumps on her arms and body.

Billy Ray stopped swimming when he heard her say she was turning blue. Still talking out to get a response to let the gang know she was turning blue. This was the start of Mary Jo's quest for stardom. She felt that all of the planned adventures that the gang was going to enjoy because of her, they should at least give her some attention.

Nevertheless, the gang was having too much fun to be bothered with Mary Jo antidotes. Billy Ray could not believe what this girl had just said. What movie did she get those lines from? She is turning blue. Unlikeable chance Mary Jo would turn blue, B. J. thought. Her skin color is not the color to even let those words cross her lips. He laughed at her making such a statement. "Does she really thing that we are so dumb that we do not know what she is doing."

For the most part, the gang could not believe their ears. The leader, the speech maker, the planner, and the smart one was standing on the edge of the water, singing a sad song "It is too cold," the gang could hear her say. She was shivering and a right to be cold standing under the tree. There was not one speck of sun light even coming through the branches.

Finally realizing she needed to move into the sun to stop making those loud sounds with her teeth, she stood in the sunlight and her body begin to warm-up.

"Huh!" Billy Ray thought as he got out of the water. This girl came all the way down here acting like she really wanted to swim. There she stands looking at the goose bumps on her arms.

At that moment, Billy Ray noticed Mary Jo looking at the twins. He took the opportunity and ran up behind her. All at once, he pushed her into the cold water. "Pooh, pooh, pooh," he could hear her say as she was coming up out of the water trying to talk. Wiping the water out of her eyes, she took her fist letting Billy Ray know, he was going to get the what for beat out of him.

Nobody could be madder than Mary Jo is right at this moment. All she could think about was Billy Ray's mischiefs act. She continued to wipe the water off her face and catch her breath. Billy Ray had not heard the last words from this girl. She would get him back.

In the meantime, Billy Ray could not leave well enough alone. He was laughing and telling Mary Jo what a weird look she had on her face when she hit the water. This did not set too well with Mary Jo. Billy Ray, of all people, could not afford to laugh at anyone. He had to go stir-up the hornet's nest instead of 'leaving while enough alone.'

"It's not funny, Billy Ray. You need to learn what is funny," Mary Jo said in harsh way. By this time, he had really stirred her up. He was about to get the tongue-lashing of his life. Mary Jo was standing in a perfect place in the creek. This was like standing on her soapbox. She put her hand over her left brow, ranting and raving as she had a fiery look in her eyes.

She was beating the palm of her hand and pointing out, "first of all I could have drowned and been dead. Second, my poor mama would be crying her eyes out. Third, it would have been your fault, Billy Ray. Now you see it is not that funny. You of all people should be ashamed of yourself."

However, she did not refer to what he did that was so shameful. Billy Ray really tried her patience. He shook his finger at Mary Jo and nonchalantly giving her the, so what gesture.

Trying to make her even madder, he splashed some water on her. Quickly, swimming away from her laughing at what he had accomplished. Billy Ray floated on his back and pretended he was a whale blowing water out of his mouth. He was having fun all by himself.

Mary Jo composed herself and was very hurt and disgusted. She softly called out letting Billy Ray know, that she "would not have pushed you into the water like that." This really touched Billy Ray's heart as he stood up in the water. Immediately, stuttering and feeling Mary Jo's pain apologized. It was just a boy's thing called 'funning.' Billy Ray told Mary Jo. He was not trying to hurt her, went over, and helped her out of the water.

For a moment, everyone was feeling how Mary Jo must have felt. To break up the moment someone yelled, "Come on, gang-back into the water!"

You could see the little bodies flying through the air into the cold water. They began to splash, turn flips, and jumped off the big rock. The gang was having a good time. They played at Red Clay Hill Creek until they were too tired to move. Billy Ray was the first to climb out of the water. He neatly spread his T-shirt out to lie on. The sun felt good on his cool, wet body. "Boy, oh boy," he said, "I could stay in this spot forever." He could feel the sun penetrating his wet body. "Ah, ah ah, h-h-hh! All was well now." The gang was at peace with each other as the lazy days of summer was spent.

CHAPTER XI
THE GREAT CHALLENGE

The twins chose to stay in the water and pretend that they were boats. They were going through the water blowing bubbles with their mouths. Shirley wanted B. J., to look at her swimming like a fish and holding her breath for ten minutes.

In real life, she only held her breath for thirty second. Shirley put her head under the water, and continued swimming back and forth.

Finally, she came up gasping for air. She then wiped the water off her face. "See! See! I told you I could hold my breath. I bet I held it for ten minutes, too. You can't even do that little Pudding," Shirley said.

B. J. was not going to let this little girl out swim him. He took the challenge but had forgotten that he wore glasses. B. J. let this little girl trick him in to doing the impossible. He did not have any swimming lessons, and definitely swimming with his head under the water and without his glasses on was a no-no.

Shirley was trying B.J.'s patience as she called him the forbidden name, "Mr. Smarty Pants." All the girls seemed to get a joy out of calling B. J. smarty-pants. This only created bad vibes with the boys, who sees the girls as pests.

Mary Jo, looking at the twins swimming, noticed that little B. J. did not have his glasses on, and really cannot see very well. Nervously, thinking, he's attempting to swim without his glasses on. The child is almost blind, as a bat. You would think that he would know that by now?

B. J. attempted to prove to Shirley that she was wrong. He tried to do the impossible. He held his breath for a couple of seconds. The twins, still in the water, looked at B. J. trying to beat Shirley by holding his breath longer.

It did not go well with B. J. because all at once, he was springing up out of that water like a whale. He was jumping up and down, up and down, trying to catch his breath. He forgot while still under water trying to get his breath. He swallowed a mouth full of water.

Simple Pleasures

You could hear him making those loud choking sounds. He was acting like a person taking his last breath. He was fighting the water trying to keep his head up. Poor thing, it was hard for him to fill his lungs with some air before he would go back under. He came up again wiping the water off his face and gasping for any kind of air.

Mary Jo, being of sound mind, took charge of the situation and yelled for Billy Ray. He was busy splashing around in the water and did not see B. J. At that moment, Mary Jo yelled as if she saw a snake. She pointed to B. J. "Go get that boy out of that water Billy Ray before he chokes to death."

B. J. was having a hard time, struggling and fighting the water. Mary Jo jumping up and down for Billy Ray, "to get him out the water."

"B. J. get out of that water before you drown yourself. He's always trying to do things that he cannot do." Mary Jo continued to say.

It was time for Mary Jo to step up and handle the problem. She put one hand on her hip. The other hand she used to point her bony finger. She became their second mama again. She told B. J. to go with the Billy Ray. "Don't he dare try to do anything fancy anymore?"

B. J. did not try anything else. He was remembering what the twins did today. They think they are so smart. However, knowing the brain and that entire collection of Critters he owns. There will be something for both of them. He hit the water and continued splashing around with Billy Ray.

At that moment, Mary Jo was standing on the bank and reluctantly waved her hands for the gang to come on. They immediately realized what Mary Jo had planned, and got out of the water. She played on their imagination again by painting them a picture of those "big, black, sweet, juicy cherries are just ripe for the picking-hum-mm-mm."

With that thought in their minds they all quickly climbed out of the water to dry off. The air was chilly as they all tried shaking their heads. They were trying to get the water out of their ears. Then the thought lit up like a light bulb as Billy Ray said, "Oh, that's right. The heat from a rock will draw the water out of your ears." Immediately, Mary Jo searched around and found a rock. Touching the rock for heat she slowly put the hot rock to her ear. She could hear her ear pop and felt the water running out. "Boy, Billy Ray," Mary Jo said, "that really works. I can hear now. Thanks a lot."

The gang hurriedly dressed and ran down the road. They were making good time when Mary Jo, their great leader, decided to find out if B. J. and Billy Ray could climb a tree. Billy Ray, feeling a little perturbed, spoke up and said, "We're boys, aren't we?"

He flexed his little chest and made a muscle with his bony arms. That just made matters worse as Mary Jo shook her head. With her hands on her bony hips swaying from side to side, she said, "What that got to do with climbing a tree, huh? Cause you are boys?"

Billy Ray refused to answer Mary Jo. She threw up her hands saying, "You are impossible to talk too, Billy Ray. I don't know why I punish myself like this."

Billy Ray being defensive and beat on his chest like Tarzan said, "For Pete's Sake! Give us a little sense, Mary Jo. What boy do she know cannot climb a tree? That's a man's nature thing to do is to climb and be wild." She just gave up on Billy Ray as she gave him one of those looks.

The gang continued walking down the road in the hot sun towards those big, black sweet, juicy cherries. No one said anything as the gang imagined how the cherries looked. The cherries were just hanging there waiting to be pick. The gang would pop the big juicy cherries in their little mouths.

Finally, they all tried to talk at one time saying how many cherries they were going to eat. B. J., cautiously reminded them of the last time all of them got sick. But then, a thought came into his mind to get back at the twins. He told the twins because they are smaller than the rest of the gang. They could eat as many as they wanted too.

The twins were elated knowing that they could do something that none of the gang could do. It was if a hush had come over the gang. Everybody was in their own little world thinking about the cherries. None had really eaten anything since breakfast and their stomachs were making weird sounds.

Breakfast was used up swimming at the creek. The empty stomach will soon need something to fill it. What would be a better treat than those big black juicy cherries to satisfy their hunger?

Everyone enjoyed themselves playing at the clay hill and going swimming at the creek. This truly was a full day of fun. Mary Jo really knew how to plan some fun things for them to do.

The sun seemed to be getting hotter as the gang made their way up the road. Their thoughts were still on their prize cherries. They had a determined look on their little faces. It did not matter that the sun was beaming down on them, they were on a mission.

Simple Pleasures

CHAPTER XII
THE BLACK HAWK CHERRY TREE

Mr. Henry had worked for the old white couple that had willed to him ten acres of land. On these acres of land, Mr. Henry had a little fruit stand on the side of the highway where he sold his prize fruits.

He had never married so there was no one but him. The little house where he lived was painted white and trimmed in green. It had a big porch with a slider swing and a couple of chairs on it. As the gang approached the house, Mary Jo noticed a figure sitting on the porch. To her amazement, it was that old nosy Mr. Sam sitting like he owned the place. This old man was about a hundred years old. Most people knew him as the town's gossiper and porch-sitter. He wore the same old tired, brown, faded-out Stetson hat and outdated pinstriped suit. His cane had an eagle head carved for the handle. The tip of the cane was gold. He always wore a pair of Stacy Adams shoes and would proudly get them spit-shined every Friday morning.

They said that he paid 'no never mind' to whose porch he sat on. He just dipped his snuff and spit all over people's yards. It was hard for him to keep any snuff in his mouth. There was not one tooth in his mouth. When he opened his mouth all you can see for days was his pink gums.

The older people said that he used to be a dandy or ladies' man. He could out dress the preachers. However, not too many of the young people liked him around because he smelled like old stale tobacco and that once-a-week Saturday night bath was not killing that six-day musk.

Mary Jo eyed the old buzzard, while she stood with her hands on those two bones she called hips. "Don't he have a house to go to? Mr. Sam is always sitting on other folkies' porches like he owns them. Huh! To go a little farther he spits that old Sweet Garrett Snuff on their grass. Everywhere you look he leaves brown spots. Its really a shame that he does that to mostly everybody in town."

Billy Ray disagreed with Mary Jo as he spoke up, "Oh! He's just old, that's all."

Mary Jo, being impatient, was waiting for Billy Ray to finish what he was saying. She stopped and looked at Billy Ray in disbelief. While they were in deep conversation about Mr. Sam, he was well aware of their presence.

Mr. Sam noticed the gang as they were walking up the road. He hollered, "Hay, hay, hay, hay, gangbusters. Where do yoes think ya going? Dose yo mammys knows yoes up here?"

"Oh my goodness," Mary Jo said, stunned and knew that 'old snuff-dipping, nosy-Butt' Mr. Sam will probably tell her mother he saw us up here. I will have to worry later knowing myself, I will figure a way out she thought.

This could have put a big damper on their cherry picking. What were they going to do now? They did not come all this way for nothing. Something or somebody had to give and it wasn't going to be the gang.

Mary Jo had enough, and enough is enough as her facial expression let the little gang know she would take care of the matter. She walked over to the porch and looked Mr. Sam straight in the eye. B. J., Billy Ray and the twins were too chicken to go over to the porch. They stayed near the road waiting to see what was going to happen.

Suddenly, Mary Jo decided to do a performance worthy of an Academy Award. She boldly told one of those lies that her mama said was cussing. The gang stood there with their mouths dropped almost to their knees in amazement. Mary Jo told old man Sam that Mr. Henry sent them down there to pick his cherries. They could have a few when they finished picking Mr. Henry's cherries. For a moment, her own gang believed what she was saying to Mr. Sam.

Mr. Sam started to laugh and said, "That shor was nice of yo chillin to does dat for ole Henry."

At this time B. J. walked up and whispered in Mary Jo's ear as they were going to the backyard. "Boy, Mary Jo, we are really going to get it now. You know old man Sam is going straight to our houses and tell."

Mary Jo put her hand up as if to stop B. J. from breaking up her plan. She felt a chill as she took time to let B. J. know he was spoiling everything now. "Just get yourself ready for these cherries. Hum, I can taste them now." Mary Jo said.

This did not faze B. J. as his glasses continued to slide down his nose. He tried and tried to tell them they should wait until Mr. Henry came home. His hand began to sweat as he nervously leaned against the cherry tree.

Mary Jo was wondering what that boy was waiting for. "Why! Is he not climbing up that tree to get us some cherries?"

Billy Ray could feel Mary Jo's eyes staring at him as he wiped his hands on his pants. He quickly shimmied up that tree like a squirrel.

Shirley looked over at B. J., looking like he was scared of his own shadow. This was all Shirley needed to see as she stood on her soapbox picking at B. J. She was having fun calling him a baby and taunting him.

Sandy, being annoyed and disturbed, said, "Why don't you leave B. J. alone, Shirley? He has a right to be afraid. In fact, we should start thinking about getting our hide-in tan, too. Because when old Sam the man gets through telling it with his busybody, nosy self, we had better have a good story. For the most part, we had better get ready for those switches and our hide-ins tanned."

By this time, Billy Ray had found a big limb loaded with the big, sweet, black, mouth-watering cherries. He got on those branches and began to shake and shake and shake, until cherries were all over the ground. The ground looked like it was a carpet made of cherries. All under that big tree was the little gang putting handfuls of cherries in their mouths. They were popping those cherry seeds out as if they were bullets.

"Hum, hum, hum!" Are the sounds that could be heard as Billy Ray stayed up in the tree getting his fill. Billy Ray was happy that he had the gang getting their stomach full of those sweet, juicy cherries too. However, what happened to those kids after a while was unfortunate. The only sensible one in the gang was B. J. He tried several times to stop the gang from eating too many cherries. They would not listen.

"No-oo-oo!" They paid B. J. no never-mind. Now they would have to suffer the consequences. Billy Ray was laid out on the ground holding his stomach. He was groaning something terrible. All you could hear him say was, "Oh, Lord! I am going to die. Please somebody help me," was the poor pitiful cry coming out of his mouth.

CHAPTER XIII
JOY THEN PAIN

The twins were just as pitiful. "OOOH, OOOH!" They moaned and groaned holding their little stomachs. They were crying for their mommy. Shirley and Sandy were crying, thinking it was the end for them. They were going to die and their mommy and daddy weren't even in town. The twins were in bad shape as they pleaded, begged, howled, and cried aloud for some relief. Mary Jo could not think of anything but go and relieve themselves. She did not know where Mr. Henry's outhouse was located. They needed some help to stop the pain. Poor little twins continued to moan and groan like a baby calf that have lost its mama. Well! Mary Jo was in just as bad a shape as the gang; she had to put on that pretend face as if she was alright. Through the moans and the groans, they all needed to go to the bathroom.

But the twins cried out knowing that they cannot make it home. It is too far and we will be a mess by the time we get there. They need some relief and not too soon. Their little stomachs felt like a big size balloon that was ready to burst.

Oh, to feel their mother's soothing hand crossed the two little girl's minds. Her touch would make the pain go away as it continued to hurt. The noise of the moans and groans sound like a choir tuning up to sing. The joy and happiness that the gang have before while eating the cherries have turned into pain and suffering. Their great leader had to come up with something and fast.

Mary Jo knew that Mr. Sam would soon come around to the backyard. The little gang was making so much noise that the people down the block could have heard them. This would be all that Mr. Sam needed to see the twins laid all out under the tree crying for their mama. Billy Ray crying out that he was going to die because of the pain in his stomach. Between the aches and pains Mary Jo had to help her friends. After all, she was their leader, and this was her plan.

By this time, Mr. Sam decided he would come around to the back yard. He wanted to investigate all of the noise he was hearing. Lo and behold there, spread out on the ground,

Simple Pleasures

were the "Mighty Gangbusters," the big Black Hawk Cherry Tree conquerors. Mr. Sam was spitting snuff everywhere. He was wiping his mouth with the back of his hand and started laughing and slapping his leg at the sight that was before him.

"Well, I never," he said. "Yose chillin done gone and eat too minny dem cherries. Yes, sir-re, shore I'm borne."

"OOOOh!! Mr. Sam," cried Billy Ray. There was not any need for Billy Ray to ask the old man for any help. This is all Mr. Sam wanted to see was these poor kids in misery. The pleads, the begging and the help me, did not faze this old man. He had something on them to run and tell their parents about what they did. He knew the kids were not dying. He was enjoying the moment looking, teasing and downright being mean to the gang.

Mr. Sam knew what the boy was going through. This brought back memories of times when he was a boy and the same thing happen. He was in somebody cherry tree eating too many cherries and suffer the pain too. But he was not giving the gang any sympathy. Mr. Sam was enjoying the gang's misery and pain.

He pointed his old thin finger and told them to hush their fuss. "Ya not dying. Yose was mine chillin I'll take dat there stick to yose hidin, shore wood. Yose jusin got de flexes Ah! Hun Yose will be all right." They just need to go down to double seater once and for all.

Mr. Sam held up two fingers indicating the outhouse with the moon and the stars caved out in the door down near the alley.
Mary Jo took charge of the situation. She told the twins to follow her down to the double seat. However, Mr. Sam saw a moment to tease the girls. He said, "If in I was yo gals I take a stick."

The twins were in too much pain to realize what he meant. Laughing at the girls, Mr. Sam told them about those spiders and other critters that might be in the there. He didn't make things any better; he started laughing again.

Sandy tried to be brave, but everyone knew she was scared to death of spiders. There were other things that crawled she did not like. Sandy took Shirley's hand and told her to come on as she picked up a stick to kill the spiders.

Shirley ate too many cherries and was in a worse way than the others were. She had to walk bent over almost walking on her hands down to the double seat. She tried to cry but the pain was so great she couldn't even do that.

They could hear the cries that Shirley was doing as she promised herself, she would never put a cherry in her mouth. "Never, never, never," could be heard as if this was going to stop the pain.

This looked like the end of the gang's great adventures. Their plans for the summer seemed to be over, finished. Who would want to tackle another fruit tree? The proof was here. All you could hear were the pitiful sounds of pain and moans. The twins made their way as best they could on down to the double seat. Mary Jo suggested that the twins could share one of the seats and she would take the other. She ensured the twins that they would feel better when they relieve themselves of their misery.

B. J. was just standing around looking at all the things that were going on. There they were moaning and groaning and holding their stomachs. They want some help so they could get some relief. Mr. Sam decided that he would leave them in their misery. He was walking faster than his cane. One should wonder why he was in such a hurry. He went down the road like he needed something. Billy Ray finally got his turn on the double seat. He sat groaning and wondered was this worth the pain.

"Oh! No it hurts, it hurts. I'm going to die; I just feel it." Billy Ray groaned.

Mary Jo yelled, "Billy Ray, you are going to be all right in a minute and stop all that talk about dying."

Finally, Mary Jo, Billy Ray and the twins got some relief. They were walking very slowly down the road toward their houses. The gang was so sick from the cherries that all they wanted to do was to lie down somewhere. There was not an ounce of energy left in any of them. They all wanted to hurry on to their houses. The little gang was to meet at Mary Jo's house about ten o'clock the next day.

However, little did she or the gang know that Mr. Sam had made it to their houses "spilling the beans." He figured out that Mr. Henry didn't tell them to pick those cherries. They just flat out told the biggest lie going Mr. Sam figured out. "Huh! Shore dos," as if he was talking to someone.

By this time, Mary Jo had made it home. She slowly climbed up her steps to the porch. She opened the screen door very slowly entering the hallway. Mary Jo felt a little better as she walked to the kitchen.

Simple Pleasures

CHAPTER XIV
SPILLING THE BEANS

Mary Jo made a sudden stop in the doorway to the kitchen. She was surprised when she heard voices and could not believe her eyes. There, sitting at the table with her mother, big as you please, was that old man Mr. Sam. Mary Jo darted through the doorway before they could see her.

The big brown icebox would be her cover. Sitting near the back door was the icebox, this is so the iceman could bring the ice. Most of the time he would leave a trail of water when he came through the house. All the women, in town would make the iceman go around to the back door.

She quietly signed and slowly peeped around the icebox. Mary Jo had a good view of Mr. Sam. He was gesturing with his hands. Her poor mama listened and continued to nod her head and say, "Uh Hun, Uh Hun, Uh Hun, shore nough hum."

Mary Jo could not believe what she was hearing. The old man Mr. Sam was telling her mama a bigger lie than what she told him. She knew not to tell a lie even though she had told Mr. Sam one. That was a three-letter word, that her mama would tan her hide for. Her mama, told her that telling a lie was cussing and God do not like "cursers." Then she thought, I have already said "the curse word." She put her hand across her mouth murmuring. "Oh! Oh, Oh, Jesus forget me." She really was trying to say, forgive me.

Mr. Sam sitting at their table, telling the story about how Mary Jo, was the leader of them "poor chillin," and how she "brought them chillin over to Mr. Henry's house to steal his cherries." He was nodding his head and hitting his hand as he went on telling her mamma how bad that girl of her was acting. "And it beat all I ever see. That gal of yose shimmied up dat tree so fast dat I thought it was a squirrel. Uh Hun. Shore did."

At that moment, Mary Jo felt the need to rescue herself. Like Superman she leaped out from the side of the ice box scaring Mr. Sam. It scared that poor man so bad that snuff was going everywhere. He tried to get his breath after swallowing some of the snuff and was choking.

Mary Jo, so overcome by the scene that she fell on the floor. She was laughing so hard while her poor mama was trying to help Mr. Sam. He was trying to get his breath back as the snuff was spilling out of his mouth.

Mrs. Finney gingerly patted him on his back. Finally getting his breath and composure back, he gave Mary Jo a look that would have killed a snake. His brushy eyebrow lifted and with a frown on his face, murmured something to her mama. Mary Jo could make out a little of what he was saying. She did hear him say, "she needs her hind-in take to that there stick, and she won't bes going around stealing. Un-hum, shore dose."

Everything was quiet for a moment when Mary Jo's mama told Mr. Sam that she would take care of the matter. Mr. Sam shrugged his shoulders and quickly made his way out the back door. You can bet he was madder than a wet hen. Mr. Sam had the last word as he was still murmuring to himself.

Mary Jo knew that she was in for it now. It really did not seem to matter too much to her. She slowly picked herself off the floor. Her eyes did not make any context with Mr. Sam or her mother. She kept her eyes fixed on the towels that were hanging on a rack. She did not dare look up because of the shame she had brought on her mama.

The big fibs she so proudly told Mr. Sam were deep in her thoughts. She could not believe that this old snuff-dipping, musky smelling man would be telling on her. What right did he have to say anything? He was not her daddy. Mary Jo did not realize that he would make a beeline over to her house. "He must have ran instead of walked."

Those long skinny legs of his got the job done. He 'spilled the beans' on the gang. *What business did he have telling on us? That cherry tree did not belong to him.* Mary Jo could feel the rage raising up in her but had to calm down and face her mama.

Mr. Sam definitely did not like kids, she knew now. There was the proof with him telling her mama. *All he wants to do is tease us kids and tell on us.* Mary Jo was trying to remember what she said that was so bad. She was in a cloud now as she imagine herself a star.

During this time, Mrs. Finney still had a problem trying to infiltrate that mind of her daughter. She is in la, la land and not even aware of what her mama will say to her. Mrs. Finney was trying hard not to be angry at Mary Jo. Her voice was soft, but she spoke with authority. Mary Jo knew that soft tone of her mama's voice meant business. Her mama was not pointing her finger or raising her voice. Mrs. Finney needed to teach her a lesson and being loud would not help her point.

However, this did not help the way Mrs. Finney was feeling at this moment. She was ready to blow her top. The thought of what Mr. Sam told her was constantly running through her mind. Hitting the palm of her hand she said, "Mary Jo yoes git over hean right now."

Mrs. Finney's words came out of her mouth as if she was ringing out a wet towel trying to get the last drop. Mary Jo was acting as if she did not hear what her mother was saying. She seemed to be somewhere else, while her body was just standing there. What was this girl up to now? She had a faraway look in her eyes. It was as if she was daydreaming like Billy Ray do most of the time.

This did not faze her mama one bit. She was sitting at that table pounding on her hands like she was kneading a piece of dough. All you could hear in that kitchen that day was the echoing sound of Mrs. Finney giving Mary Jo the what, the ifs and the for.

"Dat Mr. Sam could have wrote a book in de time it took fore him to tole me what yose did. And Mary Jo, ya and that Mr. Sam just a wasting my time. Ya see me trying to canned dis hean green beans. I ain't has no time to give fore yore foolishness, ya hean," her mother was saying angrily.

After hearing what her mama was saying about Mr. Sam, Mary Jo was scared stiff. She began to wonder what was going to happen. She humbly said, "Yes ma'am, mama."

She did not dare question her mama at this time. Mary Jo had to come up with something and fast. While Mary Jo was deep in her imagination, she did not hear her mama ask her another question. "What was you doing shimming up a tree? And girl don't yas lie to me, heah,"

Mary Jo sadly and lowly let out a pitiful "Yes ma'am, mama."

Nervously, Mary Jo went into her act like she saw at the movies. Instead, of telling her mama what really happen. She explained her first point, she did not shimmy up the tree like a squirrel. It was not the right information that Mr. Sam stated. Billy Ray climbed the tree. He shook the tree, so that the gang could get some cherries. This girl was set on convincing her mama that she did not do anything wrong. Mary Jo, using her two fingers to make her second point said, "Mr. Sam was not in the backyard during this time. He was sitting on somebody else's porch spitting that brown snuff in their yard. And, and the third point I like to make is, when he came around to the backyard, Billy Ray was on the ground. His stomach was hurting bad. He was asking Mr. Sam to help him. He was crying about his belly hurting, but Mr. Sam just wanted to get the gang in trouble."

CHAPTER XV
MAKING A POINT

Mrs. Finney was not at all impressed with Mary Jo trying to explain herself. She listen to Mary Jo's every word, then quickly interrupted her, wanting to know, "What what kind of gang?" Her mom really got it wrong about the little gang. She informed Mary Jo, "you better not bes with them troublemakers. Has you lost your cotton-picking mind? And in noes certain terms yoe noes get away with dat. I's got something for dat toos. Yoes means yoes trying to be with little troublemaking. Ain't I's tole yoes time and time agin not to bes hanging around bad kids? Did I's tole yoes dat, Mary Jo?"

Mary Jo, the great speaker, seemed to be at a loss for words and struggled to give an answer to her mama. She was like an echo saying the gang's name. "Oh, oh, no, no, mama! Billy Ray, B. J., uh, the twins uh, uh, Shirley and Sandy and that's all."

She hurried up and came to her senses and was pleading for her life. She dropped numbering her points and explained to her mama. "You know the kids I play with that attend church with us."

The poor girl could not hold back the tears any longer. Her tears were running down her face like a faucet. Her mama's heart hurt from the scolding and tongue-lashing she was giving Mary Jo. She looked at Mary Jo with a pitiful look on her face, "I's surprised at ya. Ain't I teaches yose better than dis? To respect other people property and be nice to older people. Huh? Baby."

Her mama's eyes began to look glassy as she hung her head down. Mary Jo remembered how her mother told her that children do not know "dat" it hurts the mothers just as much as it hurts them.

This didn't make any sense to Mary Jo. When her mama was the person giving out the scolding. Time seemed to stand still for a moment. Her mama was not saying anything, just sitting and looking at her child. Mrs. Finney had her arms wrapped around herself to find some comfort.

A pitiful rippling sound from Mary Jo's voice broke the silence throughout the kitchen. She tried once again to explain what happened but the big lump in her throat would not let her. She wanted her mama to know how sorry she was. The gang was just having some fun. They did not mean to hurt anyone. Mary Jo tried once again to swallow. It hurt to swallow, and the lump seemed to be getting bigger. Then just like one of her acts, Mary Jo fell to her knees. One would think she was going to pray. She began to cry as hard as she could. She was not feeling any remorse for what she had done. Embarrassing her mother, stealing Mr. Henry's cherries and making poor old Mr. Sam swallow some tobacco juice was enough.

    Her mama was in complete shock. Calling, Mary Jo back to her senses. "I's ain't has time fore dis kin of foolishness. Yoes nos that I's hav to put up des beans and you all wasting my time."

    All Mary Jo could say now was, "Yes ma'am, mama," sounding like a mocking bird repeating herself. While getting up off the kitchen floor and trying to make her mother feel sorry, she came up with a great idea.

    Mary Jo thought, she would do one of her favorite movie star's acts. She started acting as if her head was hurting really badly. She put her hand on her forehead and made weird sounds thinking her mama would tell her to go upstairs and lie down for a while.

    However, her little plan backfired. As Mary Jo once told the teacher, "Her mama is not a dummy." Mary Jo got the surprise of her life. She told Mary Jo she better git up off that floor and in a hurry. Mary Jo said to herself, "Ugh!! Why don't she just go on with the whipping? She punishing me with all this talking."

    Nevertheless, Mrs. Finney was not trying to be mean to Mary Jo. All she wanted was the truth. Her mama said, "Did yose heah what I said, girl?" Mary Jo was so deep in that little deviant mind of hers, she was not paying any attention to her mama, but somehow manage to grunt, "Not doing it again!"

    Her mama didn't say anything else. She went to the backdoor and pointed to her garden. Mary Jo knew what that meant; for her to pull those weeds out of the garden. This job will most likely take Mary Jo three weeks or more according to how fast she worked. Her overactive brain and foolishness has made her learn a hard lesson.

    For the most part, Mrs. Finney, don't have to worry about what Mary Jo is up to now because she will be pulling up weeds for weeks. Now, if you have never seen a garden in a little town it is definitely not like you think it is. You can go out the backdoor of a house and see land as far as the eye can see. It is as if looking at one of those cowboy's movies where they are out on a cattle drive, just open land as far as the eye can see. This is what

Mary Jo's, mother's garden looks like. She has rows and rows of plants.

Mary Jo is devastated. Staying in the yard for weeks is going to be overwhelming, especially since she is the leader of the gang. What are they going to do now?

Never mind, the little gang. It was time for her to remember the rules her mama told her. She still can see her mama hitting her hand and beating out you better not look or climb another cherry tree. "Yes, ma'am, mama." Mary Jo quietly said.

After hearing her mama lay the law down, Mary Jo suddenly felt brave. She had the nerve to ask her mama, "If the gang could meet here tomorrow."

"Huhhhhhh," her mama said, as if all of her air had been let out of her body. Her mama was getting ready to say one of those old quotes grown-ups say, "Over my dead body they will."

Mary Jo knew not to say anything else. Anyhow, that did not stop her from wondering how the gang would be over her mama's body if she's dead. *Grown-ups can say the silliest things,* Mary Jo thought.

You can bet Mary Jo's mama got to thinking about what she did over at Mr. Henry's house getting in his cherry tree. Mrs. Finney knew that Mr. Sam was going to make it his business to tell everybody on the block about what Mary Jo did. And knowing Mr. Sam he is going to add some more on to what really happen.

Simple Pleasures

CHAPTER XVI
WEEDING THE GARDEN

The heat was getting to Mrs. Finney and frustration was taking a toll on her. She was trying to get her green beans canned and this had to happen. Mary Jo knew her mama was going to preach her a sermon now. Maybe that is where Mary Jo got her talking talent from. She braced herself and then her mother started, "I's doing all I's can to keep food in your mouth, a roof over your head and clothes on your back. And havin Mr. Sam tole me something like dis, yoes gonna outside in dat garden."

Mary Jo had forgotten all about how tired and weak she felt. Slowly she walked out the door when her mama said, "Take dat look off your face. Yoes not grown yet. Trying to sass me, your mama, with them eyes of yores."

By this time, Mary Jo was saying so her mama didn't hear her, "I wish sometimes my mama would just go ahead and whip me because it only hurts for a little while. The pain seem bad at first, but if you rub it a bit it doesn't last that long. I know I was wrong, but she keeps on talking about what she would do to me. Words hurts worse than a whipping."

Mary Jo hung her head and went on out the back door. There facing her was that great garden her mother loved. You could bet a quarter her garden had tons of weeds that needed her immediate attention. Hanging on a big nail just outside the screen door was an old straw hat. Mary Jo took the hat from the nail and flopped it on her head. She thought, at least I can have a little shade. Mary Jo stopped and remembered she had better get some water to drink. She eased herself back into the kitchen and quickly got some ice put it in a jar of water. Mrs. Finney went back to canning her green beans. Mary Jo was glad that her mama didn't bring up what she did again? She eased herself out the screen door and down to the garden.

Her mother had planted a big vegetable garden. It would take a week just to go down one row she thought. She really got mad at herself, kicking at the dirt and gravel on the ground. This did not help her situation any, she still had to pull weeds.

The sun was not giving her any break either, because this time of day it is really hot. Most people are trying to find a cool spot, but Mary Jo had to pull weeds out of her mama's garden. Her mother has a handyman that comes around on Saturdays to weed out the garden, but That is no help to poor Mary Jo now.

It was one of those days where you could lie under a big tree drinking lemonade, hanging out with your friends and looking up at the sky to see how many animals one might spot or maybe just be quiet and listen and hear the sounds of summer. The birds would be chirping high up in the trees. The insects would be humming as they buzz in and out of the flowers, smelling and tasting the sweet nectar from the wild honey sucker plants. The cool breeze would be blowing softly across her face, while thinking what would be good for the gang to do tomorrow.

Mary Jo smiled, thinking the fun the gang had going swimming, getting and eating too many cherries. The fresh air must have gotten to Mary Jo because she did not realize what was before her. Soon reality will set in as she began to talk aloud. "I'm always getting myself into some kind of trouble. No friends around to help me pull some weeds. Here I am all by myself," as she stomped her foot in disgust.

She hit the dirt as hard as she could, looking for some peace. Mary Jo was having a temper tantrum out there all by herself. She realized how foolishly she was acting. Very slowly she bent down on her bony little knees. The many weeds were before her, so she began to pull all the weeds that were taking over her mama's vegetable garden.

There was not any reason to be mad. She did the deed and now she had to pay the cost. A song was in her mouth as she decided to sing to make things better. She pulled up everything with her nimble fingers that looked like weeds.

The more Mary Jo sang the better she felt and forgot about everything. She stayed in that garden until the sun was about to go down. The evening breeze rippling across her sweaty body as the lightening bugs came out flickering their light. All the other night creatures started singing their songs. The light dew of the night was like a wet blanket, engulfing her tired little body.

She was so engrossed in what she was doing that she had completely forgotten about the time. It seemed not to make any difference to her until she heard her mama calling her to come to supper. Mary Jo stopped and looked at her little hands all dirty and gritty. Her fingernails had so much dirt under them that she could not see where her nails started or ended. She slowly walked back up to the house and thought, "Were those cherries worth all of this?" A big smile crossed her face. Her tired little body made an attempt to jump up. "Well, yes it was," she loudly cried out.

Simple Pleasures

    She stopped at the door where her mama kept a pan of water and a bar of lye soap on the windowsill. Mary Jo carefully washed all the dirt and grime off her hands and gently washed her face. The aroma that was coming from the kitchen made her hungry. Mary Jo slowly entered the kitchen and said, "Mama, I'm sorry for what I did today." Mrs. Finney walked over and gently hugged her and said, "Sit down and eat child, yore supper is getting cold."

    She slowly pulled her chair out and quietly sat down to eat. You could hear her take a sigh of relief and think what a day this has been. Mary Jo knew that her time out in her mama's garden was light compared to how she had let her mama down. Her behavior was uncalled for, and she deserved every bit of the time she had to weed the garden. Mary Jo sat quietly enjoying the dinner her mama had made for her, she thought, *I have better things to do when my time is up from the yard.* A smile crossed her face as she looked back on the events of the day. This was something she would see at the movies.

CHAPTER XVII
THE SUMMER RAIN

The bedroom door creaked as Mrs. Finney quickly and quietly tiptoed out of the room and down the stairs to the kitchen. Mr. Bill, one of Mrs. Finney boarders, would get up early. He would go downstairs to the kitchen, make a fire in the stove, and put the coffee on. The aroma of the coffee sitting on the back of the stove filled the air. Mrs. Finney opened the back door and the freshness of the morning air flowed throughout the room. The rays of sunlight gaily danced off the windowpanes, making rainbows of colors across the red plaid tablecloth on the kitchen table.

A thought crossed Mrs. Finney mind as she started to remember the many times she was working in them fields and pulling weeds, All day long in the hot sun for a little money. It was really hard on the body because of all the bending over she had to do. She said to no one in particular, "I noes de pain dat little girl of mine went through."

Nevertheless, she had to teach that child of hers not to go around stealing and then lying, especially to older folks. She thought, *that is all that old man Sam wanted to see them chillin do. It was if he wanted to have something to tell de folks in town.*

Putting her hands on her hips, Mrs. Finney said, "Um! Now dat shore beats everything. Mary Jo Ruth over there taking Mr. Henry's cherries. Um, um, um, and it shore did not belong to her."

She laughed as she thought about Mary Jo pulling those weeds and not having to whip her behind. She quickly reached over and taking the big black iron skillet off the hook and put it over the hot stove. She tested the fire, it needs to be good and hot. She poked and stirred around the coals. The fire was getting just right as she noticed the poker getting red hot. Mrs. Finney had decided to cook Mary Jo's favorite breakfast, country ham with red gravy, grits, eggs, and some of those delicious peach preserves. There were homemade biscuits with that good country butter melting and running down the sides of your fingers. "Uh Hun, uh hun, uh hun, that shore is making me hungry just pondering about it," Mrs. Finney said.

Mrs. Finney was reminded that Mary Jo is all she got now. Her daddy been gone a long time now and the two of them are going to make it. She wiped her hands on her apron and began to roll out the dough for the biscuits.

Then, with a song in her heart, Mrs. Finney began to sing. Her voice of song was so powerful around that kitchen, Mary Jo who was stirring by this time, quickly got up. She hurried to see what was wrong. Her feet did not seem to move fast enough as she went down the stairs and into the kitchen trying to figure out what wrong with her mama.

"Mama! What the matter?" She asked.

She looked around from her Kenwood Double Oven cast iron stove that burned wood and coal saying, "Child yoes never mind. Go and git your clothes on and come to breakfast yoes heah."

Mrs. Finney was happy down in her soul. She could remember a time when it felt like her world was caving in on her. Her thoughts went back to the time when her heart was heavy and her spirit was downcast.

It seemed like only a few days ago when Mary Jo's daddy was killed working on the railroad. She was devastated when the railroad company man came and told her about the accident. She was big with Mary Jo and due in a month. However, that same night she went into labor, some of the woman from the church came over to be with her. Dr. Johnson was called and Mary Jo, tiny little thing, was born.

Mrs. Finney laughed as she thought, maybe dat's why dat girl is so darn smart. She had a nerve to come too soon. Well one good thing came out of my heartaches was Mary Jo, and oh, Lord, forgive me, dis house. The railroad gave me three thousand dollars and I brought a house.

Mary Jo hurriedly used the bathroom, washed, and had those clothes on before you could say, "Come and get it."

The smell of the food alone could almost make you hurt somebody, an old expression when something tasted good. Mary Jo and some of the menfolk in town knew that her mama could cook mud pies and make them taste good.

Just the smell that country ham simmering in that red gravy filled the air and make you eat until your belly was about to bust. You could hear that girl coming down those stairs two and three as if a bad dog was chasing her. The hunger pains were moving around in her stomach and she needed to get to her plate and fast.

She rushed over to the table that was under the kitchen window and took a seat. Mrs. Finney walked over to the table with her plate. Quickly, taking the plate, Mary Jo took her spoon and started shoveling that food into her little mouth. She just looked at Mary Jo, and her daughter knew what that meant. Slow down before yoe choke yore self, heah.

She did manage to ask, though the bites, if she could go over to B. J.'s house for a while. Mrs. Finney knew that it was time to let Mary Jo go play with her friends. However, her mama laid the rule down again to Mary Jo. The whatnots, the fors and don't yoes darn.

Mary Jo knew this rule now as she knew her left from her right. Nothing or no one could change her mind on anything. She definitely has learned the hard way. She looked at her hands and nodded her head that she understood. Mary Jo knew the rules like she had to remember her name. On her brain's dos and don'ts were permanently written. If she forgot or attempt to forget, her little hands and fingernails would bring her to her senses.

Mary Jo had the plan for their playhouse to be in the empty space down near her mama's chicken coop. She asked her mama through her eating a piece of ham if it would be all right. She said, "Long as you don't bother with my chickens, scaring dem to death."

"Yes ma'am, mama," Mary Jo said.

She finished her breakfast and was out the door. She did not wait around to give her mama a chance to lay down anymore of her rules. Mary Jo was happy to be out of the yard, most of all from pulling all those weeds. Looking at her little hands again, she could see her fingernails again. They are pink looking and actually had some feeling back in them, that is the way she wanted them to stay. She rubbed her hands and vowed she would never again pull weeds again.

Simple Pleasures

CHAPTER XVIII
WHY TODAY?

The blue in the sky was slowly turning darker as she heard the roaring of thunder. "Of all the time it has to rain, why today." Mary Jo said. Then as if, she had some power over nature she demanded the rain not to come. She had a need, and it was to get to B. J.'s house.

She was acting as if the rain was going to answer her back. Hurrying down the road, she noticed the birds flying towards the trees. The clouds were completely dark, then Mary Jo came to her senses and realized that it was about to rain. "What the heck?" She said. "Even the birds know it's going to rain."

Mary Jo had not walked that far when she saw B. J. coming up the road. He had his head down looking unconcerned. He was kicking at the dirt and rocks with his hands in his pants pockets with his favorite beanie on his head.

This little hat had some character and style to its looks. There was a baseball pin collection that neatly went around his beanie. The little propeller that looked like a toy airplane turning in the cool breeze. It was placed right in the middle of the hat ready for take-off.

The sound of hearing his name suddenly got B.J.'s attention. He looked up from the road and saw it was Mary Jo calling him. He began to run toward her waving his hands. He was so happy to see Mary Jo again.

Immediately, B. J. started asking her questions, "What're you doing?" Mary Jo was glad to see B. J, he saved her time and a long walk to his house.
B. J. was bothering his mama and she told him to go find his friends and play. So he decided to head over to her house. Mary Jo was just happy to go be with her friends after her mama laid down the law.

The very thing that Mary Jo did not want to happen, happened. It began to sprinkle as she was letting B. J. know that she was glad his mother ran him off. She did not want to walk all the way to his house if it was going to rain. Mary Jo felt a big drop of rain hit her right in her face, this really made her upset.

Yelling at the rain as if the rain cared. Mary Jo was not pleased at all. She did not feel like getting wet and then the sun would come out and she would get dry. The rain would make the weather hot and sticky and she just did not want that to happen. Mary Jo must have forgotten that it only rained for a short time, not all day. It's summer and it rains off and on.

They began to run down the road when B. J. stopped to smell the wet dirt. "Umm-mm," the sound he was making. He was acting as if he smelled one of his mama's fresh baked pies. Really getting excited he asked Mary Jo to smell the dirt. Mary Jo gave B. J. one of her looks. This did not help the matter any as he pick up a hand full of dirt telling Mary Jo he could eat it.

"Oh, stop talking crazy, B. J. You know dirt is nasty," Mary Jo said, feeling annoyed. This only brought on more conversation from the great scientist. He knew about the dirt and at one time or another everybody have eaten some dirt.

Mary Jo just stirred up the scientist mind. Realizing what she did, she decided to let him win his point. After all, he might be right about eating dirt, Mary Jo thought. He has so much knowledge on a lot of different things. She was not eating any dirt though. She threw her hands up and continued walking down the road.

It began to look bad as the rain came down harder. Mary Jo and B. J. looked like two little wet rats with their clothes sticking to them. Her ponytails now matted to her head and looking a sight. B. J.'s little hat was soaking wet as the red had started fading into the yellow. The red and green were mixing their colors too. That did not seem to bother the little propeller in the middle of his hat. It had the nerve to be turning and blowing in the wind.

Mary Jo stopped thinking about the weather and focused her attention on her plans. She knew this plan for the gang today would not get them into trouble. For the most part, even the rain could not bother her. She knew it is good for the flowers and other things that needed a fresh drink, including her mama's garden.

On the other hand, B. J. started to wonder and look somewhat puzzled. He was hoping Mary Jo was not doing one of her hairbrained plans that was going to get them in trouble again. The gang definitely did not need to do something like before. He hit his head as if he was trying to get a point over. "We are not going to do any of Mary Jo's brainy plans and that is it." B. J. said to himself.

Mary Jo, still feeling good about her plan, noticed how B. J. was looking and acting. His glasses were on the bridge of his nose and was looking over them as if he could not see. Mary Jo paused, trying to decide whether she should tell him or not but said nothing. B. J. still had that look of confusion as he waited for Mary Jo to tell him the plan.

Being the type of person she is, Mary Jo had to act out what she had to tell B. J. She was swaying from side to side with her hands on her bony hip, popping her lips and slowly said, "Well! I will tell the gang something great. The gang is going to have a playhouse. We can build a playhouse today."

B. J. did not give Mary Jo a chance to finish. He let out a big, "Wow! That's a great idea, Mary Jo." He stopped being happy knowing the gang does not know the first thing about building a playhouse. Mary Jo could see the look this boy had on his face.

Finally, it stopped raining. The rain did not help the temperature none at all. It got hotter and humid. Mary Jo felt like they were in a steam bath as their clothes were trying to dry. Mary Jo squeezed her top out and wanted to know if B. J. got a whipping.

"No, Mary Jo. I told Murdear that I was trying to stop y'all. You, along with the others continued to eat the cherries until all of y'all were sick at the stomach. Did you get a whipping Mary Jo?" B. J. asked.

CHAPTER XIX
MARY JO'S MOMENT

This was Mary Jo's crown and glory moment to tell somebody what happened to her. Mary Jo promptly said, "My mama had me pulling weeds out of her garden for a week." She hit the palm of her hand, saying she could not go anywhere but to church. "I had so much dirt on me until you would think I was doing one of those soap commercials, you know, the one that comes on the radio that talks about taking a bath every evening."

B. J. nodded his head as if to agree with what she was saying. "You didn't like that huh, Mary Jo?" B. J. asked, smiling. Knowing how this girl like to perform B. J. should have left that question along. She began to really act very proper and poised saying, "Oh, oh," as if she suddenly was feeling some pains. "B. J., it was all right taking a bath. At least I got all that gritty dirt off me because, B. J., girls do not," popping her lips again, "like to be dirty like boys." She went on to tell him that boys do not take a bath until Saturday nights. They somehow forget about the other days. Oh! I forgot, not unless you boys go swimming, that's the only other time your body sees any water."

B. J., clearing his throat like he had something caught in it said, "Ah, Rah, ah rah Mary Jo," as he reminded her that boys and men do not need that much water on their bodies like girls. B. J. was really proud of himself for such a brilliant response.

Brilliant or not, that did not set to well with Mary Jo. She was all puffed up with her hands across her brows and flipped her hand at him. B. J. was smart this time. He saw the opportunity to change the subject and talk about her ordeal in her mama's garden. He knew that Mary Jo's mama garden was as far as a little eye could see.

This was not an ordinary garden that would have a few rows but a large field with rows and rows of things growing in them. B. J. knew Mary Jo, had to pull weeds out of that garden. He just wanted to keep on the good side of her. "Um, I know you glad to be out now? You was in jail girl," B. J. said smiling. She sensed that this conversation was not going anywhere. She decided to not say anything else, thinking it's better than getting a whipping with those old switches.

Simple Pleasures

Them switches won't let you sit down for a while, your hind-in would be hurting so bad. B. J. was still waiting for Mary Jo to finish telling him about her ordeal.

However, pure pleasure was staring B. J. in the face. The rain had left puddles of water in the sink holes in the road. B. J. was about to play, jump, and romp in every hole that was filled with water

This was the time to seize the moment and started playing in the mud puddles. He would run and jump in those holes so it would splash. Like a little kid he would burst out laughing. The boy was enjoying himself and did not have a care in the world.

Mary Jo, looking disgusted, could not understand why boys think that every mud puddle they see need to be jumped in.

B. J. was having so much fun as he glanced over at Mary Jo. There was laughter and joy coming out of his mouth. He tried to get Mary Jo to come and join in the fun. She let B.J. know that she was already wet and did not need to add muddy water to her clothes.

This did not stop B. J. as he continued to jump from puddle to puddle, laughing and having a good time by himself. Nevertheless, this did not sit to well with Mary Jo, as she gave B. J. the look and walked on down the road to Billy Ray's house.

Unexpectedly, nature boy saw a lizard darting out from the tall grass. Mary Jo saw it too and started hollering. This girl is always wanting the boys to kill little innocent creatures. If it was left up to Mary Jo, every little bug or critter would be dead. B. J. was having too much fun chasing that lizard down the road. He had no intention of killing innocent critters that God created. He is a scientist, and was paying Mary Jo no never mind. She was a sight to see jumping up and down, up and down like a cheerleader at a game hollering at B. J., "Kill that darn snake, kill that snake."

Finally, the lizard ran across the road into the tall grass. Mary Jo was so done with B. J.'s behavior that she started acting like she was his mama. Putting her hands on her hips and swaying from side to side like her mama does. There she was scolding him again, letting him know he should have killed that snake. She did not mean for B.J. to chase after it like some wild man.

By this time, B. J. let Mary Jo know that it was not a snake but a lizard. He laughed so hard that he almost wet himself. B. J. stopped and realized that he had to go and bad. Looking at Mary Jo and wanting her to tell him what to do; he knew that it wasn't any use thinking he could hold it until they got to Billy Ray's house.

Mary Jo, being smart, pointed her finger to the tall grass swaying in the soft wind. Throwing up her hands, she stepped aside, and B. J. helped himself to the tall grass.

B. J.'s hollering made a bold statement that sometimes, Mary Jo, was impossible to deal with.

She was so peeved at B. J. and did not wait for him. She walked as fast as she could until the poor boy had to run to catch up with her.

Immediately he confronted Mary Jo. B. J. was so put off about her being so smart and so afraid of everything. He just could not understand this girl and her behavior. B. J. is so smart too, that he does not realize that both of them think on the same level. She is just as smart as he is but in different things.

B. J. stopped and took a good look at Mary Jo and wondered if Mrs. Finney acted the same. She had to get it from somebody. *The next time I am over to her house I will study Mrs. Finney and see if I can come up with some answers.* B. J. must have lost his mind, he knows children are not supposed to stare at grown-ups. Coming back to his senses B. J. thought about something else.

Simple Pleasures

CHAPTER XX
GIRLS ARE SPECIAL

This girl should go to acting school after all, Hollywood needs characters like her, he thought. She could pour it on as she reminded B. J. that girls are special. "God intended for girls to be like they are, to be afraid of bugs, snakes, and all them other things."

B. J. was dumbfounded, wondering where is that found in the Bible? B. J. should have never even let that cross his mind. He did not get a chance to ask her. Mary Jo jumped right in, taking charge of the situation. She brought up the fact it is stated in the good book.

Mary Jo has two cents' worth of knowledge about the Bible. This is all she needed to prove what she said is right. Mary Jo remembered the time that she shared this information with B. J. It is in the book of Hezekiah. B. J.'s mind went back to the time this girl said the same thing. He threw up his hands and realized that it is highly impossible to outthink this girl. B. J. just let her be right and did not have anything else to say.

Finally, they got to Billy Ray's house. B. J. went through the gate and up to the porch calling Billy Ray. Billy Ray came around from the back of the house. He was looking up on the porch. Some of the planks on the porch were missing. There was cardboard up on the windows, the screen doors falling off the hinges, and the house in a bad need of a paint job.

Billy Ray said, "What are you doing here B. J.?"

"Oh, there is Mary Jo over there leaning on the gate," B.J. said, not answering Billy Ray's question. She was standing and wondering, why Billy Ray's daddy did not fix up the place. Mary Jo did not like going up to Billy Ray's house because it looked so bad. She did not say anything to Billy Ray about his house and continued leaning on the gate.

Billy Ray waved at Mary Jo. She threw up her hand slightly giving him a wave. B. J. could not wait until they were all together. He grabbed the opportunity to do the honor of telling Billy Ray that they were going to build a playhouse today. Sounding over excited, B. J. explained to Billy Ray, "That is the reason we come to get you?"

Billy Ray face lit up as he anxiously asked his mama if he could go with Mary Jo. Like most mothers, Billy Ray did not receive the answer he was expecting. At that moment, you could hear his mama telling him she need him there to "help with the younger chillin."

Simple Pleasures

"Boy, that all you think about is playing," Billy Ray's mama replied. B. J. slowly backed off the porch and made a beeline down the steps. They waved good-bye and did not believe that their friend could not come. Mary Jo noticed the big disappointing look that B. J. had on his face. She did not know what to say to him. She felt that Billy Ray needs to have some fun like they were planning to have that day. Mary Jo was sad at that moment because they needed Billy Ray to help bring the playhouse together.

While feeling down and sad, B. J. and Mary Jo heard Billy Ray calling them. At that moment, B. J. and Mary Jo's eyes lit up like Christmas tree lights when they saw their friend. Their little hearts were overjoyed wanting to find out what happened.

Mary Jo was the first to ask, but it was plain as the nose on her face B. J. thought. His mother just changed her mind. He was there now and so happy that his mama let him go play with his friends. They went down that road locked arm and arm as three peas in a pod. Just happy being with each other during this summer.

Mary Jo, B. J., and Billy Ray were feeling good at this time. Billy Ray did not know what to say but, "Wow!" He let Mary Jo and B. J. know how happy they made him. It was just great having Billy Ray, their friend, to share in the fun they were going to do Out in the hot sun, three friends decided to make a pact to be friends for life. They all agreed to include the twins when they got to their house. Mary Jo was getting excited about making a pact that would last. They need too first find a safety pin, or something they could prick their little fingers with. Being bold, she wanted to find out who had a pin, Billy Ray quickly answered her question?

Thinking he was still in school or at church, Billy Ray raised his hand up saying, "I do, I do, and I do in my pants pocket. I put it there just in case my shorts start to fall down on me."

Mary Jo did not want to ask Billy Ray if they were his daddy's shorts. She noticed he had his shorts folded over the top of his cut-off jeans and knew they was not his. Anyway, to stop Mary Jo from asking him where his shorts was. Billy Ray shyly gave her the answer that he did not have any.

B. J. turned out to be a true friend. He put his hand on Billy Ray's shoulder letting him know that he had plenty and would share with him. This is what a true friend would do.

Mary Jo overcome with gratitude reached over and gave them a big hug. She told B. J. that was so nice of him to share. Billy Ray, with tears in his eyes, let his friends know that they were the best friends any guy could ever have. They all agreed it would be friends for life no matter where they were.

They were rounding the corner when Mary Jo saw the doctor's car in front of the twins' house. She began to wonder when the twins' daddy and mama came home.

B. J., knowing now that Mary Jo could not leave her yard to know that they were back. He saw the doctor's car over at the Ford's house last week. A whole week lost in that garden and she missed everything. She did not get the chance to listen in on grown-folks' conversation.

Out in that field her mama calls a garden, Mary Jo missed the hot gossip. When the gang's mamas had company over to their houses, the children had to scram in a hurry. Children knew that they did not have any business sitting around listening to grown folks' business. They had to take their leave in their room or outside.

Sometimes the children would sneak near the door so they can hear what the grown-ups were talking about. However, Mary Jo missed the chance of knowing that Dr. Johnson and Mrs. Johnson came back from their vacation.

She grinned because she did not know anything else to do. Billy Ray knew he could find out what the women were talking about from that nosy Mary Jo. She could definitely give you the facts on everybody. While walking up the walkway to the big white house, Mary Jo started laughing at the thought of her being so nosy. The three friends made their way up the steps and reached for the doorbell. The twins quickly ran to the door and were happy to see their playmates. There the twins stood full of life and ready for the time of their little lives.

Simple Pleasures

CHAPTER XXI
THE GANG IS HERE

The twins were so happy that the gang was here, Mary Jo, Billy Ray, and B. J. Coming up the walk, the twins could see them and wanted to be the first to welcome them. The twins had decided to surprise the gang by open the door before the bell rang.

Mary Jo was expecting to see Mabel staring down at her as the door open quickly. Instead, the twins were at the door happy to see Mary Jo. She wondered if their mother was sick because they did not give her a chance to ring the bell. Casually, she wanted to know if their mama is sick. Sandy quickly responded, "Oh no, nothing like that Mary Jo, we've been getting on mama's last nerve." Like most mothers she needed the twins to go and play, or find something to do besides asking her questions.

Shirley adding her two cents' worth that their mama felt as if she was on one of those people on a quiz shows, on the radio. Mary Jo decided not to say anything but nod her head. She knew what their mama was going through with the two of them. They are full of questions. Shirley shyly let Mary Jo know they would not ask any questions today. She patted the twins on their cheeks and gave them a hug. However, before Mary Jo could tell the twins the plan for the day, Billy Ray blurted out, "We are going to build a playhouse, twins."

The twins, looking somewhat confused, wanted to know, "out of what? We do not have no money to buy some wood to build a playhouse." Sandy said.

Mary Jo had to reassure the twins that she was thinking about going to Ford's appliance store. "Maybe we can find one of those boxes that an icebox came in"

Billy Ray knew that would be the very thing they would need. The bottom of the box have wood around it to protect the motor. It is the idea thing for a playhouse. Mary Jo remembered that's how the box was made when her mama bought an icebox.

While the gang was getting their plans together, the twins went to ask their mother if they could go over to Mary Jo's house. The twins went running through their house calling their mama. Mary Jo, B. J., and Billy Ray stood looking lost.

Mabel was cleaning the window on the door. The gang noticed how strange

Mabel was acting. They could hear the twins running down the hallway to the front door.

Mabel said, "Wait a minute, twins," as she held her hand for them to stop. They were in a hurry and Mabel is standing there like she is on police duty. She looked out at kids, but did not say anything. She continued wiping the window on the door. "I'm getting through with this here window, ok?"

The twins looking at Mabel with a scornful look on their faces. Of all the times, why did she have to clean the window now? Seeing the look that the twins had on their faces she stepped back and motioned with her hand for them to come on. She reminded them to be back by supper.

Mabel decided to have some fun and suggest that they could stay and wash the window on the door. The twins went quickly pass Mabel and out the door. They were happier than two peas in a pod jumping up and down. B. J., Mary Jo, and Billy Ray quickly waved at the twins again. The twins were happy now that the gang came to see them. They were ready to have some more fun, regardless of what Mary Jo had planned for them. The twins were glad that their parent was home but they were not any fun like the kids. You could feel the happiness that the twins were feeling.

Simple Pleasures

CHAPTER XXII
MAKING A PACT

Their faces and eyes lit-up in the sunlight. Mary Jo was delighted to see the twins after the ordeal she had just experienced. No more weed pulling for her, she is making sure she abides by her mama's rules. The gang was happy to be together again and go find their playhouse.

Earlier, Billy Ray gave Mary Jo the safety pin that he had in his pocket. Mary Jo suggested that this was a good time to use the pin. They wanted to make a pact for life and do it right on the porch.

The twins were standing and looking confused. Mary Jo quickly stopped them from asking any questions. She knew once they got started it was hard to stop them. Patiently explaining to the twins, she let them know that the pin was to prick their fingers. They would bleed a little and press their fingers on each of the gang's finger. Everyone agreed this would be a great idea. The twins were smiling and wanted to go first. They bravely held their little fingers out to be pricked. However, Mary Jo whispering to them that the pin need to be clean. They wanted to do the thing right and needed to burn the pin so it would be clean.

You know it always has to be a smart mouth in the bunch to give you the rules about matches, Mary Jo was thinking as she listened to Billy Ray tell the twins they are not suppose to play with matches. Mary Jo did not want to be loud as she reassured the twins it would be all right to get the matches. She told them to bring two just in case one goes out.

All excited, Shirley hurry into the house to find a match. She knew just where to find a match. She was thinking this is going to be as cowboys did in the movies, burning a knife to clean it to take out a bullet.

Once in the house, Shirley snapped her fingers, remembering exactly where she could find some matches. The matchbox is on the kitchen door's face.

Mary Jo, feeling like the leader, took her spot on the porch.

In the meantime, Mabel, coming out the door on the porch asking, "What yoes still hanging around heah for?"

B.J. nudged Mary Jo in her side for her not to answer. Looking down at the little the people and putting her hands on her hips, Mabel stared at the gang. She was determine to get an answer.

Nevertheless, this gang did not have anything to say. They went into silent mode, looking up at Mabel. "Huh," she said, "I guess the cat got your tongues?"

Just as Mabel was trying to figure them out, Shirley came running out the door right into Mabel. Shirley did not realize she was standing there and Mabel was fuming as she turned around and went back into the house. Knowing Shirley saw her standing there, she questioned, "Huh?"

Mary Jo, sensing that Mabel was trying to be nosy, suggested that they should go somewhere else. They all went down the steps, happy as little larks singing in the morning. The gang was now out of earshot of Mabel and wanted to know when they could prick their fingers. Mary Jo had a plan, and told them they could do it in their new playhouse. B. J. was excited as he hit his fist in the palm of his hand, totally agreeing with Mary Jo. "That's what I was thinking. Let's go get the stuff for our playhouse."

The excitement was in the air and with smiles on their little faces they marched down the road. The gang had to go downtown to get what they need for their playhouse. Everybody was trying to talk at once, so Mary Jo suggested one person talk at a time. Billy Ray spoke up first and wanted to know if they should get a big box so everybody could get in it. Next, the twins came up with an idea to paint it. B. J. did not have anything to say but wondered where in the world did these kids come with things they were suggesting. It looks as if B. J. did not understand. After all, this is going to be the gang's future playhouse. Mary Jo began to wonder if this was such a good idea. The twins and Billy Ray wanted to fix up a box but did not know if it's a box made of cardboard or wood? The twins and Billy Ray was talking about dragging the box around in the alley looking for junk.

Mary Jo, with that stare of hers sternly said, "We are not going to look for anything now. The box is what we need to get first." Their leader had to put a stop to all the silly none sense. Immediately, she called the gang together and explained that they should go get their prize box first. They all agreed. The gang was trying to go to Mr. Ford's store before it got too hot. However, just ahead of them, trying to put a damper on their plans, was Mr. Sam. It is a good thing the gang had already decided to go through the alleys first. Going downtown on the street, they would most likely run into Mr. Sam. They knew from previous experiences he would be wasting their time. The alleys had a lot of short cuts and were determined to get it the job done. Their minds were fixed on building the playhouse and Mr. Ford's appliance store had what they needed. Nothing was going to stop them now. They were five little people on a big mission.

Quickly walking down the road to Ford's Appliance Store. This was the day that they could find a big box with a wooden bottom. Old Miss Daisy, one of the town's "upper class white folk," was getting one of those new kinds of stoves. This stove was the top of its model with everything on it. Mabel, who also worked for her three times a week, told the twins' mother that Miss Daisy would get her stove delivered today.

In the meantime, Billy Ray was excited about how much fun they would have playing in their playhouse. The twins had other ideas and wanted to hunt for things in the alley to put in the playhouse. For the most part, that was a no-no, with what the twins wanted to do. Mary Jo definitely had other plans. Trying to find out her plan was like looking for a penny that dropped down the sewer drain. This was her time and the gang would look up to her, after all, she felt she was a good organizer and a leader.

CHAPTER XXIII
THE PEST, MR. SAM

Just when the little gang was about to get to Ford's Appliance store, they noticed the worst person they could have seen that day. It was as if this old man followed them downtown. There he was, as big as day, with a mouth full of snuff, the pest, Mr. Sam. Mary Jo was so annoyed and beside herself as she tried not to look his way. That did not help at all, Mr. Sam was not going to leave them alone. It was as if this man enjoyed picking on these kids. He could not pass up the opportunity to hound them. There he stood, tall like a tree towering over the children.

"Well, well, if it ain't them there gangbusters. Where's does yawl think yawl goin, huh? I noes yore mannies don't noes you'll down heah, huh?"

At this point the boys quickly stepped behind Mary Jo. After all, she was the spokesperson, the leader, the planner, and the go getter. She stepped up so that she could face Mr. Sam. Without any thought with her hand shading her eyes she informed Mr. Sam that she did not have a mammy but a mama. Mr. Sam was so out done that he was doing a little jig. He was trying to come up with something to tell Mary Jo off. All the gang could hear was Mr. Sam getting choked on the snuff he had in his mouth. During this time, he was madder than a wet hen in a rainstorm. He could not speak well because his throat was still not clear. One would think after the first encounter he had with Mary Jo and that snuff, he would not try to scold her with snuff in his mouth. With his long bony finger, he pointed at the gang letting them know they have not heard the last of him.

Wiping his spit shine shoes on his pant leg, Mr. Sam decided he was wasting his time on the kids. Mary Jo just believed that Mr. Sam had completely lost his mind. "Where did he get the idea that the gang belong to him? Just because we are to respect our elders that does not give him the right to act like he is my daddy."

At the moment, the gang could not be more proud of Mary Jo than now. They did not care about her standing on her soapbox. She deserved their praise for the outstanding job she did on Mr. Sam. He'll probably be too embarrassed to run and tell the town's people what she said. When will this old man learn to stop being nosy and leave those poor children alone? He did not have anything else to do but bother the gang every time he sees them.

In the meantime, the boys were just taking everything in as they stood back and let their leader handle the situation. She always seems to use the right words on Mr. Sam. The boys were having fun looking at Mr. Sam. He had snuff all down the front of his suit coat for trying to boss someone else children.

Mary Jo was not going to let this old man run and tell on her this time. They were not in anybody's yard eating their fruit, just walking down the street on a mission. They had a plan, and it was about having a playhouse down near Mary Jo mama's chicken coop. Mr. Sam, walking slowly away from them when Mary let him know that she did not "git no beating nether." The gang started laughing and pointing their fingers at Mr. Sam.

Mr. Sam decided it was no use trying to correct these sassy kids because they had no-good manners and did not have the upbringing as his mother had taught him. He turned around, got his step together with a swag and walked on down towards town. You would have thought this man had a million dollars in his pocket, walking with His gold eagle head cane with the gold tip on it. He walked with a swag in every step he took

Billy Ray was overwhelmed as he told Mary Jo what a smart girl she was. "I bet when you grow up you going to work in the White House?"

Billy Ray could be amazing sometimes, Mary Jo thought as he stood there and shook his head in disbelief. This was her moment, and it did not faze her as she told the gang to come on. They all have things to do like find that box at the Ford's store. It was the twins' opportunity to get in the conversation. They pointed out that Mr. Sam wasted their time. "We could be at the store by now," Shirley said with a look of disgust.

Somewhat reluctant, Mary Jo did not want to talk about Mr. Sam but agreed with the Shirley. She knew Mr. Sam had already wasted so much of their time. They needed to walk faster and make up the time lost. What a sight to see, five children walking fast as their legs could take them, acting as if they were going to buy something.

However, there was not a quarter between them. Their little minds were on building a playhouse. The joy and laughter, ranged throughout that moment as if this day was Christmas. They were about to get something that would be their own as Billy Ray stopped to look in the trashcans. Mary Jo informed Billy Ray that the alley downtown does not have anything good but a lot of old junk. Mary Jo remembered that old people do not throw their good stuff away. Their best bet was to go up to Miss Daisy house to find the things they needed. "Those white folks up on that hill and roundabout have some fine things lying out in their garbage cans," She said, remembering finding a pretty hat in the trash. She took the hat and gave it to her mama. Her mama wore the hat to church and the old ladies talked about her mama. "They thought that she was being uppity with that new hat on, mama shore had a good laugh on the ladies."

The gang wanted to know why Mary Jo was laughing. B. J. was somewhat surprised that she would give her mama a hat she found in the trash can. He said, "You really did not give your mama a hat out of the trash, did you?"

Mary Jo refused to answer B. J. as she looked at him. Then she just told them she gave her mama a hat that she found in a trashcan. She felt she did not need to discuss the matter any farther. Immediately, taking her leave and walk away from the gang. She was fed-up with these nonsense question. She was determined to get the big box and get it back to their play spot by the chicken coop. "These children sometimes do not realize the importance of getting the plan finished first. Then we all can laugh and act silly once we get the box."

This girl's brain was in overtime now as she got closer to the store. The twins noticed their leader was serious. They had to run to catch up with her. The group was huffing and puffing like they were running in a race. The sun had the nerve to go behind the clouds for a minute and come back out with a vengeance. It was so hot that the heat was dancing off of the hot tar street. No one said anything but continue to walk in this unbearable heat. It was as if they did not care how hot was, the box was their goal, and a little heat was not going to stop them.

Simple Pleasures

CHAPTER XXIV
THE BIG BOX

The little town was compact with its one major department store, two five and dime stores and one bus station. They used to have two bus stations but one station moved to a bigger city. They did not have enough people going out of town. One thing one could say about the town is that the high school's football and basketball teams rode in style. They did not have to ride on the yellow buses, the teams rode on the big comfortable Trail Way buses.

The teams would get off the bus with big smiles on their faces. They felt good arriving at the schools in style and facing the team that they would definitely beat. This, indeed was riding high on the hog.

Also, there are three drug stores, one hamburger stand, and a fountain that was in the middle of the square. The townspeople and the famers would come and sit on the wooden benches to pass the time on Saturday. It could be raining, and you could go down to the square. There would be someone sitting on the bench with an umbrella. It did not matter to those town folks and farmers, it was a time to rest and let the women and children enjoy their day. The people were not concern with what the weather was going to be like. They all enjoyed their Saturday meetings downtown. The old men's joy was coming into town to hear the latest gossip.

On the other hand, Mr. Ford's store was actually before you got into town. This store was near the firehouse which faced Main Street. The police department was facing Market Street but the two buildings are to save money. When a traveling evangelist would come to town, the townspeople would look forward to seeing someone different than the local preacher.

Finally, the gang approached Mr. Ford's store. The twins were all excited as they pointed to a large box. Immediately, Billy Ray ran and crawled inside the big box while B. J. was just standing and looking. He was trying to decide whether he was going to try out the box, too. Once inside the box, B. J. motioned for Mary Jo and the twins to come. There was plenty of room for everybody. However, Mary Jo was not having any of their fun and put a stop to it.

Looking in the box and shouting, Mary Jo demand for the twins and the boys to come out of the box right now. "Oh heck, Mary Jo, we just funning," Billy Ray exclaimed. She was mimicking her teacher as she had one hand on her hip and patted her foot. Mary Jo said, in a very stern authoritative voice, "We already wasted good time on that old geezer Mr. Sam, and it's time to get the box and go."

Saying things under their breath, B. J. and Billy Ray quickly crawled out of the box. The boys were just trying the box out to see if it was big enough for them. They did not want to carry that box back to the play area and it was not big enough. Mary Jo should have waited before she decided to get on the boys' case. B. J. grabbed one end of the box before Mary Jo could start lip-lashing him. B. J. had not realized how heavy the box was until he tried to lift it by himself. He soon found out the box was no joke.

The box is heavy and he quickly let the box fall down. Mary Jo instructed each person to take one end of the box. That was the answer to their problem, with a smile, they could easily carry the box. Everyone felt a little better as each one carried their part of the box back up the alley. This was their prize possession. They could not hardly wait to get back to their play spot.

All was well for a while, but the weather was not helping the matter. It was hotter than a firecracker now. The humidity was not helping the heat either, as the twins began to whine and complain about being tired and that it was too far for them to carry box. Trying to encourage the twins, Mary Jo said, "Just think, twins, about how much fun we are going to have." This seem to help and keep the twins quiet for a while.

B. J. said, "Yeah! Twins see the white sheets hanging on that line over there blowing in the wind. The sheets are so white until they almost hurt your eyes. That is Mary Jo's sheets too. Mrs. Finney shore know how to get them sheets white, huh?"

The twins were wondering what those sheets had to do with the box? B. J. was just as anxious to sit that heavy box down as well as the twins. His hands and the muscles in his legs felt like a piece of lead. He did not want to tell Mary Jo they need to stop for a while and rest. The little gang had ran out of energy and could not wait to get that box out of their hands. "OOOOH!" That was the pitiful sound coming from the twins, while trying to see over the big box.

Mary Jo was trying to keep the gang together, after all she is tried too. Frist of all, that big box had to be placed in the yard over by the chicken coop. "Everyone can rest inside of the playhouse shortly," she reminded them.

Simple Pleasures

However, the twins were a hand full now and getting on Mary Jo's last nerves. This was a plan that all of the gang agreed to and now some were complaining. They all continued to whine and complain about the box being too heavy.

Poor Mary Jo, all she could do now was walk faster so the gang could get to the spot. They did not realize that Mary Jo's hands and arms were tired just like theirs. Nevertheless, the path was right in front of them. They were sliding and scrambling up the hill. This definitely was not a chore for the little people. They could not see where they were walking or stepping. Sometimes fate has a way of letting things happen that was not in the plan. There might be an unexpected creature in their way.

Tom, the alley cat, had a bad habit of lying on his back with his paws straight up in the air. It was as if he had to soak up some sun. It was alright for Tom to do this, but he was resting in the path. This was his daily thing, to catch some rays and play around in that area. Shirley, who did not realize Tom was there, was holding the front end of the box on the left side. She was about to experience the fright of her life. As she put her left foot down it landed hard on poor Tom's tail. That cat let out a yell that could wakeup the dead. Like a flash of lighten, Shirley let go of her end of the box.

Tom scared Shirley so bad that she took off howling and running for her life. Billy Ray sat his end down and took off running after her. He wanted to tell Shirley it was just the cat. She was running so fast that she probably broke Jesse Owens' record that he sat at the Olympics in 1936. That girl was running so fast that her feet look as if she was not touching the ground.

For the most part, the rest of the gang did not seem to care. Only Billy Ray took some initiative to go after the Shirley. The others were all trying to get to the spot. It was very necessary for the gang to put that box down. With two people missing it would be hard for three of them to carry that big box. Their leader Mary Jo took charge of the situation. She told the gang to rest a minute. They all sighed catching a breath of fresh air. It did not last very long, before Mary Jo informed them it was time to get the box over to the play spot. This did not help the problem because they still need one more body. Billy Ray was needed and in a bad way to comeback and help them. Mary Jo dragging the box while B. J. pushed. Then running up to them was Billy Ray. A sparkle of light hit the rest of them seeing Billy Ray.

CHAPTER XXV
RAIN, RAIN GO AWAY

Billy Ray made it back to the playhouse looking bewildered and tired. He was looking as if he had just ran a marathon. He was huffing and puffing, in between trying to tell them that Shirley was hitting the corner before he could catch up with her. He could not run that fast. When he got to the corner, she was running up the steps to her house.

Sandy was somewhat dazed from what was going on. She was still sitting in the middle of the path holding her end of the box. It was time for the gang to get themselves together and start on their playhouse. Mary Jo took charge of the situation and told the gang to take the box over to the empty space under the tree.

Amazed at how fast Shirley could run, Billy Ray said, "Wow! Did you see Shirley running, Mary Jo?" He was waiting for her to say something.

Billy Ray got his wish. Miss Mary Jo told flyboy that anybody with common sense knew the answer. "If," as she popped her lips "you are suddenly frightened like Shirley was, you would take off running fast, too. Shirley was just scared, and you would run fast if it had happened to you."

During time this time, Mary Jo was feeling great, she had given them a grown-up answer. She thought, girl, you are too smart. Hum!

Billy Ray was not as dumb as Mary Jo might have thought. He knew that Mary Jo could not come close to outrunning Shirley now. Billy Ray felt proud, knowing that Shirley could outrun all of them. In the meantime, Mary Jo arrogantly told Billy Ray to pick the box up and to stop talking so much.

He did not reply, as he threw up his hand in being disgusted with Mary Jo and her attitude. While the gang was busy discussing how fast Shirley could run, the weather was about to make a big change. Those summer showers were about to introduce the gang to a mighty cloud burst. In other words, thunder and lightning was about to break through those dark cloudy skies. The gang still did not have the box in the play area. They were deep in

Simple Pleasures

procrastinating and did not realize that something was about to happen. All of a sudden the rain came pouring down in big drops. Mary Jo began to jump up and down trying to get the gang to take the box over to their play yard.

Billy Ray shouted, "Everybody pull-one, two, and three. Pull hard, everybody." The gang was pulling with all their might. B. J. was slipping and falling down in the wet grass. His glasses were not helping the matter either as he tried several times to get up. Mary Jo shouted at B. J. saying, "It's no time to be playing. Get up and help us. This is your playhouse, too."

B. J. was trying to wipe his glasses as he slowly got up. The rain was coming down hard. The grass was really soaked by now and B.J. moaned as Mary Jo gave him that look. This boy was fierce and knew Mary Jo was acting again as if someone had just appointed her to act like their mama. B. J. was mouthing what he had to say to her where she could not hear him. Nevertheless, this satisfied B. J. he finally got the better of her. Out of breath, the gang got the wet box over in the space right under the big tree. They began pushing and shoving each other. Each one was trying to be the first to get in. You could hear them say. "Move! Let me in."

The lightening was streaking across the dark sky as the thunder roared. At last the little gang was safe in their haven, the cardboard playhouse. Billy Ray was the first to get in the box. He noticed the box needed some windows. After everyone was in the playhouse feeling comfortable, Billy Ray suggested putting some windows in. The gang agreed but did not have the tools to cut out windows in the box. Immediately, B. J. pulled his Boy Scout knife out of his pocket. Mary Jo sarcastically said, "Well! I never! Who would've thought you would be carrying a knife, Brains?" This was a proud moment for B. J. He expressed himself saying, "All men carry a knife, Mary Jo."

Dumbfounded, this left Mary Jo without anything to say, B. J. had finally got the best of Mary Jo. All she could do was give him one of those looks. He leaned up and took his knife out of his pocket. He carefully cut a small square hole on both sides of the box. Everyone sighed and took a deep breath of fresh air. Indeed, the rain made it hot and sticky in the box without those windows. This was their playhouse.

The rain continued to come down in between the trees. The gang did not realize that the top of the box was now weighed down with water. After all, this was a cardboard box and only the bottom end box was wood. The front end had the four flaps that you would use to open and close the box.

Nevertheless, the water began to seep through the box. The gang was having so much fun that no one noticed. The water continued to fall on top of the box and ran down the sides. All at once the roof was heavy with water. The top of the box caved in and all the water poured inside like a flood. The gang did not realize what was happening to them. They were rolling and hollering trying to get out the box. Billy Ray, who was closest to the front, dived over the top of the box.

However, just in front of the box, Billy Ray landed right into a mud puddle. B. J., who was right behind him, fell on top of Billy Ray. It was a sight, seeing the boys falling in the mud hollering like it was doomsday. Mary Jo, said, "What are you hollering for Billy Ray and B. J.? It is just water, and you are a little wet. You and B. J. are acting like you do not take baths. Huh!" Mary Jo smartly said, "The rain has done some good." The boys looked at each other and busted out laughing. They began to throw mud at each other. Mary Jo was thinking that is just like boys, playing in the mud.

It was not that happy of time for poor little Sandy. There she was, sitting in the broken down box. She was crying her eyes out and looking like a wet cat. Between the crying she would stop and say, "I want my mama, oh, I want mama and can somebody please get my mama?"

On the other hand, the boys were having too much fun to notice Sandy. Poor Sandy just sat there and continued to cry her little heart out. In the distance, Mrs. Finney was calling Mary Jo to come in out of the rain. Her mama did not want her to 'catch a death of cold,' so Mary Jo suggested the gang come up to her house and dry out. They all darted for the back porch looking like four little wet rats. Mrs. Finney came to the door and burst into a laugh. She nodded her head saying, "My, my, my, look what the rain sent me."

They were so cold their teeth were chattering. Mrs. Finney put four chairs around her kitchen stove. She gave them each a hot cup of mint tea using the herb that grew wild in her yard. "Wow!" Billy Ray loudly expressed as he sipped his tea feeling the mint aroma filling his nose, warming him up, and making him feel so good.

Simple Pleasures

CHAPTER XXVI
A SPECIAL TREAT

Mary Jo knew they were missing something but did not let the gang know. For right now, the gang was enjoying the mint tea. There was a special treat that Mary Jo would ask her mama for. It was one of those freshly baked teacakes. She could smell the cinnamon in the teacakes and taste the aroma that was lingering the in air. Mrs. Finney said jokingly, "If Billy Boy would take out the ashes from the stove, I might think about giving y'all one."

Mary Jo smartly whispered that her mama's boarder takes out the ashes every morning. She let the gang know that her mama was playing with Billy Ray. "Sit down," Mary Jo quickly said.

Her mama began softly singing and gave each of them a teacake as big as a biscuit. They all thanked Mrs. Finney as she passed the plate around. B. J. looked at Mary Jo but thought it was best not to ask. He wanted to go up to Miss Daisy's house to look for some junk. B. J. figured it out. Mary Jo did not want to be bothered right then. B. J. decided that eating his teacake right then was better than talking about junk, anyway there is always tomorrow, B. J. thought.

In the meantime, Mary Jo decided that the gang could go alley hunting. Maybe they could find some junk to put in their playhouse. Billy Ray munched on his teacake nodding his head in agreement. The teacake taste so good that he wanted another. Mrs. Finney knew that boys could eat more than one. She passed the plate around again, and the boys were smiling from ear to ear.

However, Mary Jo and Sandy had enough. They looked at the boys stuffing themselves like pigs. They did not care about what those old silly girls was thinking. They thanked Mrs. Finney again and told her she was the best cook in the whole world. Mary Jo thought those boys would say anything to get some food. She shook her finger at them and shook her head.

Mrs. Finney looking at the kids saying, "Theys always into something. Theys more busy than dem dare flies tryin to git at my food. Hun, hum shore does." She laughed and left the children to finish getting warm and eating their teacakes. They finished

91

their teacakes, drank their tea, and talked about what they were going to do on the next day.

This plan with getting a playhouse was fun until the rain came. They would have to come up with a better plan for a good playhouse. Mary Jo was thinking of getting Sandy to ask her daddy. After all he knows how to fix people maybe he knows how to build them a playhouse. There was a big if in asking the good doctor.

When was he going to find time to build them a playhouse? Sandy was sitting with her hand under chin trying to think of a good time. She then told Mary Jo that in two weeks they would be going on vacation. Somewhat, surprised Mary Jo was wondering where were they going now? She did not want to get Sandy started giving her a whole history of where they were going. Mary Jo, being nosy, wanted to know where they were going and how long would this trip be?

This lifted Sandy's spirits up knowing that her leader wanted to know where they were going. All smiles, Sandy being to tell the gang their plans for their vacation. First, they were going to New York to see her daddy folks and from there they are going to Florida. Mary Jo did not give Sandy a chance to even tell her who they were seeing in Florida. She was now acting like the twins, asking one question after another.

On the other hand, the boys were not that interested in what the girls were talking about. They were still enjoying their teacake and talking about Bill Ray's hobby (airplanes). Just the mention of airplanes made Billy Ray's eyes lite up from the pure joy of liking airplanes. Also, having a friend like B. J. who did not mine hearing or seeing an airplane.

B. J., hitting his forehead, came up with the very thing that they could do without the girls. They could have a day when Billy Ray can come over and spent the night. Billy Ray was so happy because he has never spent the night at anyone's house. He has heard how other children brag about how much fun they had. No one has ever asked him to stay over. He thanked B. J. and let him know if it would be alright with his mama. Billy Ray and B. J. said at the same time, "Friends forever."

Mary Jo heard what the boys were planning to do without the girls. She informed the boys that they could do the same thing. They would get together and have a day when the twins could spend the night at her house too. Sandy said, "Y'all boys, we can do the same thing too."

Simple Pleasures

CHAPTER XXV11
THE BIG TOE AND A HARD ROCK

Mary Jo was thinking about what Sandy had told her as she laid in bed. The twins would be leaving for most of the summer. What could the gang do that was exciting? It had to be something the twins enjoy doing.

"Oh," Mary Jo said. "I don't know what to do. We have been to the movies every Saturday. Now what is next for the gang?" She questioned, as she threw back the covers and laid at the foot of her bed. She put her hands under her chin, then she began to look at the sunlight shining through the cracks in the shade. The Big Ben clock on the night table ticking to her every heartbeat.

Mary Jo stared aimlessly at the glass doorknob. The smell of mothballs in the closet was lingering in the air. Her mama hung the mothballs on a coat hanger so the moths would not make a meal eating holes in her wool clothes. Trying to come up with something was getting harder by the day, she thought. Hitting her head to make it think did not help any. "Oh brain, come on. Give me a thought."

At that moment she jumped out of bed saying, "What's the use? My brain is dead." She hurried herself to get ready for breakfast. Maybe, she thought to herself if I eat then I can come up with something. Mary Jo finished dressing and went downstairs. Her mom was coming to get her when she met her in the hallway. "Well!" her mama said. "It's about time yoes gat up child. Yore breakfast is gitting cold."

Mary Jo sat down to eat when she asked her mama what her friends could do that was exciting.

"Exciting!" Her mom abruptly said. She could not believe this child of hers had the audacity to ask her "what dem friends of hers can do." Her mama first had to realize what her child was trying to ask. Mrs. Finney was a wise woman and she let her child know it.

"Yoes never has it so good," her mama told her.

"But, but, mama, what else am I going to do?" Mary Jo asked. Her mama slowly turned from the stove and looked at Mary Jo nonchalantly saying,

"Yose can git your friends and weed my garden," and she let out a big laugh.

Mary Jo almost choked on her food. She heard her mama say the magic "weeds." She quickly said, "Mama, we don't want to work, that's what we do when we have to go to school."

Her mama knew it was summer and kids enjoy going outside finding things to do. She was just playing with Mary Jo and wanting to see what she would come up with. This was their playing time and to get out from under their parents' feet. Mary Jo did not waste any time hurriedly eating the last of her breakfast. She decided there would not be any weed pulling on her daily agenda. Excusing herself, Mary Jo quickly ran out the door. She said, "Mama, I'm going to play with my friends."

Mrs. Finney laid the rules down again that Mary Jo would behave herself. Mary Jo reassured her mama that she would behave herself as the words faded off as she ran down the path. "I am going to be good," as she waved good-by.

The fresh smell of morning air began to clear her head to think. The big blue sky with its fluffy white clouds gave no sign of rain. Mary Jo pressed her feet into the soft powdery dirt as she walked to B. J.'s house. She thought she should ask Big God. He knows everything.

Humbly whispering she asked, "Please give me something exciting to do with the twins, huh?" Mary Jo waited patiently and listened for an answer. She remembered hearing the pastor say that you could ask God for anything.

However, all she could hear was the birds chirping, the bees dancing in and out of the flowers, a soft breeze whispering by her ears, and the sound of her heartbeat. But wouldn't you just know it, right where she was skipping was a big rock just above the ground. Mary Jo's big toe caught the edge of that rock. In the inner most part of her being she let out a holler that scared the birds out of the trees. She jumped around on one foot holding her big toe. The blood mixed with the dirt ran down her little hand.

"Oh, oh, I broke off half of my toe! I'm going to die and my mama won't know it." She looked up to heaven and disapprovingly said, "Thanks Lord. I just broke off my toe." She thought, I better take back what I just said. I am wrong as two left shoes. "Oh! Lord the Father of Hezekiah."

Then she decided that was enough. After all, He is too busy with other people and their problems. She hopped on one foot down toward B. J.'s house.

"Oh! Oh! My toe is hurting," she moaned. Easing herself to sit down in dirt again, she wanted to see how much damage she had done. Looking at her toe she could not see too much, there was too much blood and dirt.

"OOOOOh me! How silly of me not to see that rock," she cried.

Her toe was throbbing so bad until it was beating like a drum. She slowly got up from the dirt and realized that it was not getting any better. If she could hop a little faster, she would be at B. J.'s house in no time at all.

The heat of the day was bearing down on her tiny body. The pain in her toe continued to throb and get worse. However, she could now see B. J.'s house through the dust. The wind was blowing dust in little circles in the road. She now felt that it might rain after all. The wind was really stirring up the dust now. Hobbling and trying to hop on one foot was very painful. Finally, she reached B. J.'s house and pitifully began to call out his name as she came through the gate. "B. J., B. J., oh B. J., don't you hear me calling you?"

B. J. ran out to the front porch rubbing his eyes. "What? What is so important that you could not come up on the porch and knock on the door. You down there doing all that yelling for what, Mary Jo?" B. J. asked.

Mary Jo was now furious at B. J. The "uh, ah, oo-ooo-oeee," continued to come out her mouth. She tried to put her hand on those bony hips of hers but was off balance. B.J. did not have his glasses on and this made thing worse. Mary Jo was shouting by this time because B. J. was not paying attention to her hurt toe.

"If you open those two big eyes of yours, you will see what has happened to me!" Mary Jo angrily told him. B. J. looking from the porch could not see how bad her toe was hurt. All he could see was some matted dirt on her toe. Mary Jo was beside herself now thinking that is why this boy has to wear those double thick glasses. He cannot see. She was getting very frustrated and peeved. Mary Jo decided to hold her foot up so B. J. could see her half off toe. It was not B. J.'s fault that he could not see her half toe. He felt maybe Mary Jo was stretching the point, a little. B. J. was wondering where was the blood?

This really stirred up the science in him. He jumped down off the porch so fast that he scared the old dog lazily lying in the sun. There he was trying to imagine how half of a toe would look. He quickly put his glasses on all excited as the thought of how gruesome the toe would look.

It is not even near the month for Halloween for him to be acting like a mad scientist. The excitement was in his voice as he got closer to see how half a toe would look. His heart was beating faster as he looked down at her toe. "Let me see it, let me see it," B. J. nervously said.

Mary Jo, being very annoyed, said, "Of all the people in this world it had to be you. The mad, mad, scientist, coming to my rescue."

B. J. looking concerned then took a closer look at her toe. "Mary Jo," B.J. said, "That is a nasty cut you got there. I had better call my mother. She will fix it for you."

Boy wonder went running up the steps into the house. "Mudear! Murdear! Come quick! Mary Jo has broken off her toe!"

Everyone in town called B. J.'s mother "Murdear," which is short for "mother dear." She had that innate ability to mother everyone regardless of who would come to her house, dogs, cats, people, whoever, Murdear was there for them. She came running out to where Mary Jo was sitting on the middle step.

"My Lord! Child, what have yoes done?"

She slowly picked Mary Jo's dirty foot up and looked at the toe. "Hum!"

As she wiped her hands on her apron gently picking up her foot. She took a look at her toe but could not see because of the dirt that was on cut. Murdear knew she needed to clean her toe off first. She put her hand under Mary Jo's little body, carefully cradling her in her arms like a little baby. Murdear took Mary Jo up the steps into house.

Simple Pleasures

CHAPTER XXVIII
THE PAIN AND TREAT

Mary Jo was acting modest and told Murdear, "It would be all right." Even though she felt like crying like a baby. Murdear knew that she was in pain and reassured her she would take care of it. Mary Jo laid her head back as Murdear carried her to the kitchen and thought, ah! this is heaven. It had been a while since her mama has done her like this. Mary Jo quickly changed her thoughts as if someone might be reading her mind.

Anyway, she is a big girl now and do not need this nonsense. The throbbing toe quickly brought Mary Jo back to reality. Murdear gingerly put her in a chair at the kitchen table.

Like a dog sniffing out a bone, her nose perked up. The smell of a lemon-glazed cake hit her senses. Murdear had just made a cake and it was cooling on the windowsill. Her mouth began to water just thinking about how good it would taste. She had to have a slice of that cake. Hum-mm, she thought, just some crumbs would be all right.

While sitting there she had completely forgotten about her toe. She felt Murdear washing off her toe with some warm soapy water.

"My, my, my, child, that's shore is a nasty cut. Let me put some sugar on it to stop the bleeding." Many people in town knew her for her home remedies because she was part Cherokee. Her mother was Cherokee, and her father was colored. She knew a lot about the different herbs and potions for cuts and other ailments. Dr. Johnson would sometimes come calling to ask her what herb would be best to use in some of his cases.

B. J. went out on the back porch to get the kerosene oil for Murdear. During this time, Mary Jo had a puzzled look on her face. She didn't know what Murdear was going to do with the kerosene. Her little heart began to beat faster. Mary Jo thought about the cowboy movie they had seen last week. She began to remember the scene.

It was about a cowboy who had gotten shot by the outlaws. He was losing a lot of blood. His cowboy friend said he would die if the bleeding did not stop. Her mind was really racing now. She came to the part where the hurt cowboy had to bite on a stick.

A red-hot knife that had been in the fire was used to burn the wound. Mary Jo remembered that the poor cowboy had passed out. Then the cowboy who had burned him told the others, "He's alright, just let him sleep."

She was so into what she was thinking that she had completely forgotten about the kerosene. Finally, working up enough nerve to ask Murdear, Mary Jo boldly asked, "What is the kerosene for?"

Murdear had a big smile on her face. She gently took Mary Jo's little foot and held it in her hands and explained to her. "The kerosene is to keep the infection out of the cut." She poured some kerosene on the rag and tenderly wrapped Mary Jo's toe up. Mary Jo was thinking, what a kid has to go through. Now I will be walking around smelling like a kerosene lamp. Looking at her toe, she noticed that it was not throbbing anymore. Something Murdear had done really worked. Mary Jo was checking out how carefully Murdear had wrapped her toe. Then she tenderly held Mary Jo little face to her face.

"Since you did not make a fuss about what I put on your toe, Mary Jo, a nice slice of cake I am going to give you and a glass of cold milk to wash it down," Murdear said.

In the meantime, B. J. was pitiful taking all this in. He began to wonder where was his piece of cake? Murdear laughed knowing nothing was wrong with B. J.'s toe. She tenderly picked his foot up looking for a cut. "Ah, um," Murdear said, as if she found something. "Dat toe of yors B. J. don't needs my help."

B. J. thought, has my mama gone mad or something? My toe is not cut. There's nothing wrong with it. Boy, oh boy, what a fellow has to go through. All this just to get a slice of cake. Realizing what his mama was doing to him B. J. said, "But, but, but, Murdear, this is your baby boy, begging you."

"Oh! Hush yore fuss boy. Yoes going git some cake too."

Murdear gently patted B. J. on his head and escorted him to the table. B. J. quickly took a seat next to Mary Jo. Murdear walked over to the window and carefully took the cake over to the table. There she saw little bright eyes fixated on that cake. Murdear had the milk out and poured B. J. and Mary Jo a cold glass full. She cut a nice side piece of cake for them.

B. J. could see the goodie-goodie and Un hum in Mary Jo's face as she delightfully said. "This is heaven hum." B. J. mumbled under his breath and lit into that big slice of cake acting if he had not eaten in days. His mama just looked at him and shook her head. The humming sound could be heard as they took a bite of the lemon glazed frosty that was on each bit of cake.

"Hum-mm. Taste that lemon frosty, Mary Jo," B. J. said.

"It almost locks your jaws," Mary Jo said between bites.

B. J. was too busy eating to even answer her. He thought this girl talks too much anyway. It was time to be quiet and enjoy this moment. He continued to stuff his mouth. B. J. did not need to finish what he was thinking. The taste of that cake was enough to stop a lark from singing its song. It was so delicious, and that cold glass of milk just helped the cake go down so smoothly.

Getting enough of his cake and milk in his stomach, B. J. wanted to know the story behind Mary Jo's mishap. B. J. was hoping that this girl just gives him the facts. He knew she would try her melodrama on him. Poor B. J. all he wanted to know was what happen to her toe, that is all. He noticed Mary Jo taking a deep breath and sighed. She was about to go into one of her acts again.

However, B. J. sensed what she was about to do. He cleverly informed Mary Jo that this was not her time to act. In a nice way B. J. looked her straight in her eyes and said, "Just the facts okay Mary Jo?" Repeating himself once again. "Just the facts okay Mary Jo?"

Mary Jo heard those words before. B. J. got those lines from a Charley Chan movie. She could not believe he is trying to use them on her. Poking her mouth out and rolling her eyes in a sassy manner, she said "Well! Mr. Smarty Pants, just for that you want hear it."

B. J. was smart he knew that this girl just wanted him to beg. She needed to try and act as if she is one of the stars at the movies.so she can act out. He decided to use some of her tactics. He used a little drama as he pretended to be in pain.

"Oh, oh!" As if he was in pain. "Mary Jo, come on and please tell me."

This was all she needed to hear him say. Without any fanfare, Mary Jo shows B. J. the big rock sticking out of the ground and "My big toe do not have eyes." Therefore, that toe of hers hit that rock so hard all you could hear were the birds flying out of the trees, the bees humming, and a cry of pain coming out of her mouth.

B. J. was astonished and amazed but wanted to see the particular rock that had the blood all over it. This boy definitely is weird and possessed the look of a mad scientist, with his horn-rimmed glasses sitting on the bridge of his nose. B. J. was anxiously wanting to see the rock before it starts to rain and washes the blood away.

She reassured B. J. that it was not going to rain. That rock was not going any place but where she left it. B. J. was thinking, maybe this girl is smart at times. That made sense. A rock cannot get up and walk away by itself. Finally feeling good about the rock, B. J. stop being so impatient.

Nevertheless, this did not stop his creative imagination from coming up with some weird things he could do with the facts. If it was a nice spill of blood he could take the rock home and put it under his microscope. He could write up a good report on his finding. The other part of Mary Jo's toe would definitely be the prize specimen that would make his day.

CHAPTER XXIX
THE FACTS OF THE MATTER

Mary Jo calmly stood up, put her hand on her bony hips, and in earnest wanted to know, "Where did your mother get you from?" The cabbage patch?

B. J. could not believe that this girl had a nerve to ask him a question like that. He thought, who could be any weirder than she was? However, B. J. wanted to keep the peace and did with caution and waited before responding to her question.

It definitely was the rock that he was concerned about now. He wanted to find out where that rock was located. B. J. politely let Mary Jo know he did not come from a cabbage patch. B. J. informed Mary Jo, that most scientists like to look for the facts of the matter.

In other words, he went through the whole scenario of the cause and effect to any fact. There is a need to see the blood. Then maybe, the other stuff like a piece of skin. He could maybe tell what part of the rock her toe hit.

Mary Jo could not believe this boy. It did not matter to her what side, angle, or part of the rock her toe hit. As she sat there really taken back of what this boy is telling her. Mary Jo did not realize until now that this boy is what we say he is weird. He is way out there in space most of the time all by himself. She was left speechless as no words could top this boy's reason of the facts and matters of the rock. She was dumbfounded and could not believe what this boy just said. She agreed with him and put her mind towards something to do with the twins. B. J. was not really thinking about the twins right then. He was totally, disappointed with her now. It was all about the rock and the blood on it. B. J. just looked at her and shook his head in disbelief.

They finished eating the last of their cake and quickly went out the door. Mary Jo hobbled along with her kerosene bandage on her big toe. B, J. was happy now as he ran ahead of her. He wanted to hurry up and find the rock that had the blood on it.

Looking back, he called out for Mary Jo to come on. He just knew that toe was not as bad as she was acting. She can walk faster than what she is walking. It is hotter than it was when she first came over here. The sun can dry anything up right now. After all, blood is liquid and it will dry fast.

This boy said the wrong thing to Miss Perfect, as the expression goes, 'this is the straw that broke the camel's back.' B.J. was in for it now as he continued searching for the rock. Mary Jo stopped dead in her tracks and refused to go another step. She will let him find it himself, since he is the big scientist and in such a big hurry. Mary Jo rambling on to herself that, "He does not know who he's talking too." Mary Jo thought, my toe is ah, uh, well, it's not hurting bad right now.

One can see that this boy had back up to the wrong tree. He did not have the right to talk about her like that. Mary Jo was upset and refused to say anything more. She eased herself down in the grass on the side of the road.

B. J., irritated, threw up his hands and said, "Girls! Who needs them? They are nothing but a big pain." He walked down the road by himself and shouted back at Mary Jo, "I don't need you. I'll find it myself."

Scuffing his feet in the powdery dirt, B. J. set off to find the treasure, the bloody rock. The one with a piece skin on it. He was making his own self excited thinking about the rock. It should not be that hard to find with all these clues. He gritted his teeth and went on down the road to find the facts.

The mystery of the rock is deep in his mind as the sun was bearing down on him. Shading his eyes as he glanced up at the sky. "This is going to be one of those scorchers where you could fry an egg in the dirt," B. J. laughed and continued to look for that rock.

In the meantime, Mary Jo decided, she had better go help 'Wonder Boy' find the rock. In the distance she heard someone on a bicycle calling her name.

"Hey, Mary Jo, wait up!"

Still trying to figure out who was calling her, Mary Jo moved to the side of the road. She thought, this person is stone mad, if he thinks I am going to wait out in this hot sun for him.

Patience was not Mary Jo's thing because she did not like waiting. This was just too much for Miss Important. Mary Jo was thinking, I bet'u that is Billy Ray howling and waiving his hand like he goin crazy. The rider was getting closer and indeed it was Billy Ray. If Mary Jo did not step back in time, Billy Ray would have run over her with his bicycle. She howled, "Boy you almost ran over my half cut-off toe."

Billy Ray managed to jump off the bike and ran over to Mary Jo to see her toe. Looking down at her toe, Billy Ray asked her question after question. Mary Jo could not believe this boy. He did not give her one chance to answer him. Had the sun fried his brain too? She could not understand the boys. They seem to all have gone off into the deep somewhere.

The answers Mary Jo was giving him was not quite what he wanted to hear. Billy Ray wanted to know where did she get that rag from on her toe? What is that horrible smell that's his nose is picking up. To make things even worse he answered his on question. "That's kerosene that I smell. Huh, huh, Mary Jo? What that rag ya have on for?"

By this time, Mary Jo was fuming and hotter than the afternoon sun. She put her finger in Billy Ray's face and began to shake it at him. If you would have seen this girl, one would think she were their mama. Mary Jo could without a doubt be their mama, she had the role down to the finest grain of sand.

On the other hand, Billy Ray had it all figured out. Mary Jo is feeling the heat as she rant and raved over her toe. It is the toe that is now her prize possession. She took her time to let Billy Ray know the kerosene rag is on her toe to keep the germs out. "Murdear fixed my toe because I stomped it on a rock and your friend the mad scientist wanted to examine the blood on the rock." Poor Billy Ray-all alone with the girl he did not how to respond or answer her. He let Mary Jo go on with her story.

"Gee whiz!" Billy Ray finally said. "Mary Jo, that kind of hurt, huh, huh, I bet'u?"

By this time, Billy Ray and Mary Jo decided to go find B. J. Mary Jo was acting as if nothing was happening. Trying his best to help Mary Jo, Billy Ray offered her a ride. He had a bicycle that Miss Daisy had given him because he helped Mr. Bob clean out Miss Daisy's attic and she gave him the bike. He was so proud.

Mary Jo was not all that impressed with that old bicycle. She was not being nice at all by telling Billy Ray, "It's rusty and the bike is in need of a paint job."

However, Billy Ray did not care how it looked. He was so happy to have a bicycle. Mary Jo could see that Billy Ray liked the bicycle regardless of what she said about it. She said, "Okay, Billy Ray, the bike is so nice. Let's go."

Billy Ray was happy as he offered Mary Jo to climb on the back of the bike. She hesitated but carefully climbed onto the back of the bike. She was definitely making sure Billy Ray didn't hurt her toe. Billy Ray leaned a little so he could put both his feet on the pedals to balance the bike.

One could only wonder why Mary Jo was not holding on to Billy Ray. She fell off the bicycle and landed right in the dirt. Billy Ray was furious with her as she sits there acting as if she was something special. Mary Jo did not give Billy Ray a chance to get on her case.

She immediately dusted herself off and walked proudly down the road. Billy Ray picked his bike up and rode pass Mary Jo as fast as he could pedal. He was riding that bike like the ghost rider in the movies. "Now you see me and now you don't" He stirred up so much dust that left Mary Jo without words. And her anger floating through the air like the dust Billy Ray left behind.

Mary Jo was left hobbling in the dust but was making her way to the twin's house. She did not walk fast because her toe was still hurting when she tried to put pressure on it. At the moment, her mind was on trying to figure out what to do with the gang. For her to be as smart as she is it should not have been a problem.

It was hot and she did not want to lose her strength and energy on coming up with something exciting to do. She cleared her thoughts and decided to enjoy the moment without those pesky boys. A cool breeze blew her way, and she was enjoying the quietness and the sound of summer. She could still smell the oily rag on her foot but did not seem to bother her now. It was the time being alone with her thoughts that she could think about what would be good for them to do.

Simple Pleasures

CHAPTER XXX
A FRIEND INDEED

After leaving Mary Jo with her hurt toe, Billy Ray was riding his bike as fast as his feet could pedal. At this moment his thoughts were on finding his friend. Billy Ray did not have to go far before he saw B. J. standing in the middle of the road. He was looking confused and downright mad.

Billy Ray rode up and wondered why this boy was just standing there. It was hot and there was not a breeze stirring anywhere and especially in the middle of the road. B. J. must have known what Billy Ray was thinking. He knew he was looking somewhat foolish in the hot sun, in the middle of the road. Quickly, the smartest boy in the gang had to redeem himself. With his glasses at the tip of his nose looking like a scientist, head turned slightly, he let Billy Ray know the story behind the rock. The rock that broke off a piece of Mary Jo's toe is right here.

Actually, Mary Jo just stomped her toe on this rock. B. J. knew that most of the kids in town don't wear shoes during the summer. They wore shoes or sandals when they are going to the movies, church, or downtown to shop. Majority of the time the kids stomped their toes. B. J. pointed to the rock and there was just a little blood on the rock. What a big disappointment for this kid who loved blood and stuff. Trying to turn things around for his friend, Billy Ray decided to come up with something they could do. He offered B. J. a ride on his bike and went down the road. They could look for some lizards that did not dodge the car and got run over.

B. J. slowly responded to Billy Ray's idea. Sounding excited, Billy Ray pedaled as fast as he could. Billy Ray had not given up on helping his friend get over being disappointed. "Hey, maybe the gang can go bike riding one day, huh, B. J.?" Billy Ray said.

B. J. was not sounding to enthusiastic about the idea. He suggested that he talk to Mary Jo to see what she thinks about it. Billy Ray nodded his head, agreeing with his friend. B. J. started feeling good when he realized that for once he was not walking. The wind felt cool on his face as Billy Ray pedaled. B. J. was wondering if Mary Jo did not let Billy Ray ride her on his bike, after all, she had a hurt toe. He decided not ask Billy Ray, who was enjoying his bike.

The boys were not having any luck today. The road was dusty and not even a dead fly was there. It was fruitless for B. J. to continue on his quest to find any creature that was run over by a car. He told his friend to go by his house first.

"I have something that I want to give you, Billy Ray."

He really started pedaling fast heading toward B. J.'s house. All you could hear was the clanging sound of the old bike. He rode liked something was after him. Finally getting to B. J.'s house, Billy Ray gently laid his bike down and was planning on waiting outside. However, that was not what B. J. had planned and took Billy Ray by the hand and led him into his house. B. J. called out for his mama to let her know he had come by to get the bag. Murdear called back to him from the kitchen to tell him it was in his room.

"Tell Martha I said hello, Billy Ray, and I will be talking to her soon." Murdear said.

"Yes, ma'am," Billy Ray said as his voice echoed down the long hallway.

B. J. motioned with his hand for Billy Ray to come up to his room. He quickly followed B. J. up the stairs and into his room. The room was very large and had lots of books and collections of different insects and bugs. Billy Ray was acting like a kid in a toy store. He was so excited and could not believe what this boy had in his room.

Actually, B. J. had a science lab set-up like the one you would see in a movie. He was astonished at what his eyes were beholding. This kid knew a lot about science. Without a doubt Billy Ray understand now that his friend has a mind of a scientist.

At that moment, B. J. really made Billy Ray feel good when he told him that he was just like him. B. J knew how much Billy Ray loved airplanes and he could name every one of them he saw. Billy Ray enjoyed the compliment but had some doubts about being like B. J. His friend was the smartest in their class and he definitely was not that smart.

B. J. saw the pitiful look Billy Ray had on his face. He asked Billy Ray a question that he knew that Billy Ray could answer. "How many people you know can name as many planes as you can?" Billy Ray tried to think of someone but could not come up with one person.

B. J. mumbled "Uh, uh, uh, I don't know anyone myself."

Billy Ray was in a state of shock thinking that B. J. was just joking until if finally hit home. Billy Ray bust out saying, "Gosh lee, I am smart, huh?"

This is a proud moment for Billy Ray, to know things that others do not know or not interested in. B. J. made his friend feel good about himself and patted him on his shoulder. It's a precious moment when two friends complements each one's good points. They shared the joy of being friends and knew how to be proud of what they know. B. J. went into the closet and took out the bag for Billy Ray. He was standing in the middle of the room still amazed at all the things he saw when B. J. walked over to and gave the bag to him. With a big smile on his face, he waited for Billy Ray to respond.

    Slowly looking in the bag, Billy Ray was surprised at what B. J. had given him and humbly thanked him with a big smile on his face. Billy Ray was thinking it was time to go. He knew that the girls would be waiting. The boys did not have to say anything as they walked across the room. They hurried downstairs and out the door to the twin's house.

CHAPTER XXX1
THE PLAN

In the meantime, Mary Jo was slowly walking a little behind the boys. She had not thought of anything great for the twins and the boys to do yet. Her plan was to do things the twins enjoy doing. Mary Jo was at her wits' end trying to think of something. Anything would do right now. She sighed, realizing there was not anyone to help with a good plan. What can she do now?

Suddenly a bluebird flew over her head. It was as if an idea dropped out of the sky. It finally sunk in what Billy Ray had said. Miss Daisy had her attic cleaned up. What did that mean? It meant treasures! Boy, what a good idea! We can all go alley hunting, she thought.

Billy Ray and B. J. were casually standing in front of the twins' house when Mary Jo quickly approached. "Oh, you made it Mary Jo," B. J. nonchalantly said.

The boys were acting as if she had them standing out in the sun waiting for hours. However, this did not stop Mary Jo from calling B. J. the forbidden name. "Yes, Mr. Smarty Pants. Where are the twins?" She arrogantly asked.

The boys were lost for words at that moment. B. J. was mumbling something under his breath. "Uh! Ah, uh," B. J. was saying with his hand under his chin. Quickly trying to come up with something, he told Mary Jo that, "We uh, decided to let you go in and get the twins. Since you have the plan for us today."

B. J. let out a sigh of relief because he convinced Mary Jo to believe him. Pushing past the boys, Mary Jo was very irritated. She went through the gate and up to the porch. Mabel was busy as usual, cleaning the front door window. Mabel, looking down at Mary Jo, said, "Whata yoes want?"

However, Mary Jo was beside herself as she thought, Mabel, give me time to catch my breath, I might tell you. This was not what Mary Jo had on her mind and did not want to tell Mabel anything. So, she stalled for time and hoped that the twins would hear them talking. She got her wish because soon the twins heard Mabel talking to someone. They came running to the front of the house. The twins saw Mary Jo and said, "Gee, it's so nice to see you. Where are the boys you? They didn't come with you?"

Mary Jo thought these girls always ask twenty-five questions. They never let you answer before they ask another question. Mary Jo motioned with her hand for the twins to stop asking so many questions. The twins agreed to be quiet and listen to Mary Jo, they were acting like two little church mice. Mary Jo was sounding as if she really had a lot to tell the twins. The moment of glory as she was on her soapbox. Clearing her throat as if she was about to bring a message she let them know what the plan is. "We know how you twins like to go alley hunting. That is what we are going to do today," Mary Jo proudly said with a big smile on her face.

The twins loved going looking for junk in the alleys. They could not wait to go. Mary Jo told them to go ask their mama if they can go out and play. Then she leaned in and whispered, "Don't tell your mama what we are going to do, okay?"

Mary Jo knew that Mabel was trying to listen to what she had said. She acted as if the twins were going over to her house to play. Mabel continued cleaning the windows. To break the silence, Mary Jo decided to be nice and asked Mabel, "Is it fun cleaning the windows?"

Immediately, Mabel stopped what she was doing, put her hands on her hips and said, "Miss smarty, wait outside for the twins."

She opened the door and said, "Mary Jo, that's what's wrong with yoes smart and sassy gals. Think yoes can ask grown folks questions. Huh not me."

Mary Jo took the opportunity to roll her eyes and sticking her tongue out at Mabel when she was not looking. If Mabel saw what she did, the old switches would be on her behind tonight. She laughed to herself knowing what she got away with as she waited for the twins to come back.

B. J. howled, "What's taking so long, Mary Jo?"

She said, shaking her finger at him. "Hold your horses, okay!"

Finally, the twins came running out of the house with Mabel saying, "Slow down, yoe hear?" However, the twins just kept on running down the steps to Mary Jo.

B. J. wanted to know from the twins, "Where's your red wagon?" Excitedly, Shirley showed B. J. to the backyard. There under the porch was the red wagon. He had to bend down a little to reach under the porch to pull the wagon out. Shirley was trying to figure out what B. J. was going to do with the wagon. Shirley decided to be on good behavior and not ask any questions. Mary Jo would not be able to give her the "look" now.

B. J. could see the look on Shirley's face. She really wanted to ask him what was the wagon for? It was the twins' daily make-up to ask a lot of unnecessary questions.

B. J. smiled as an idea crossed his mind that the twins were writing a book. Maybe, they are trying to get some facts about a story to write for the newspaper.

Nevertheless, Shirley was being outsmarted; he did not give her a chance to ask him. He abruptly stated the wagon was to carry their treasures in. Sandy was walking to the front yard with B. J. pulling the little red wagon. The twins were getting excited, but Billy Ray was more excited than they were when he found out that the wagon was for their treasures. He loved rummaging through the trashcans in the alley.

This was the time of year that people in the town began to throw out their junk. The towns' people would be preparing for the winter months. The old fruits and vegetables that were canned a couple years ago would be the first to go. The outgrown clothes that no one could wear, the worn, cotton-filled mattress and the broken chair that someone never got around to fixing would all be there. This is what made their hearts beat faster, to go look for those treasures hidden in the alley.

So many things they would find, like the old bicycle that a child used to ride but now has outgrown. There could be a doll or two with one arm, a button eye, or missing clothes; and the forgotten rusty sled that hung in the old barn waiting for a child to ride down the steep hill near the church.

As the gang stood there, Billy Ray was crossing his fingers in hopes that maybe somebody threw out some paint. He could use it to paint his bicycle to make it look better. Mary Jo seemed to be reading Billy Ray's mind of finding some paint for that old rusty Bicycle and laughed. "That bicycle of Billy Rays' needed more than some paint." She just wanted to find things that she was interested in. She could see that Billy Ray need a new bicycle, as a smirk crossed her face.

Mary Jo getting back to more important things spoke up. "We will go up to Miss Daisy's house first. Billy Ray already told her that he helped old Bob clean her attic out the other day. We definitely can find some good stuff up there on that hill. That's where the rich, rich white folk live."

Simple Pleasures

CHAPTER XXXII
THE ALLEY HUNT

There was excitement in the air and happy faces as the gang agreed with Mary Jo's plan for the day. This was to top all other missions they had done, The big alley hunt. Mabel was standing on the porch with her hands on her hips shaking her head. She was wondering what in the world "them chillin was up to now?" The gang walked down the street with the red wagon. Mabel, still looking puzzled at what was the little red wagon for because it was too small for them to try to ride in it down a hill. She was totally, dumbfounded trying to figure out where they were going. Mabel, shaking her head, said, "Hum, hum, hum, hum," as she went into the house wiping her hands on her apron.

Billy Ray looked at Mary Jo and asked, "What are we going to do with the junk we find, huh?"

Mary Jo, a little disgusted and somewhat bothered with Billy Ray's nonsense said, "Perhaps we can sell it to Mr. Bob, the junkman, Billy Ray OK!"

B. J. mumbling just wanted to find things they could fix their playhouse with. Since the big rain, all they have now is an old, trashed cardboard box with the wooden bottom half on. Mary Jo refused to ask him what he was mumbling about so she continued walking faster towards the alley.

They picked the perfect day to go alley hunting. A breeze was blowing through the trees and down the alleyway. They were happy rambling through those big cans looking for stuff.

Mary Jo found a big bag with some summer dresses in it. She knew that Billy Ray's mama could not buy too many things for herself with all those children she took care of. She opened the bag and looked the dresses over. The way she was looking at the dress you would have thought she was downtown shopping. The dresses were almost new looking and decided to give them to Billy Ray.

She walked over to where Billy Ray was looking at some old comic books. Lightly, tapping him on the shoulder and handed him the bag. Looking surprised, he hurriedly took the bag and looked through it. He pulled out a floral summer dress that would look nice on his mama. A tear ran down his cheek as he looked up at Mary Jo. He did not want to cry as he said, "Gosh, this is so nice of you Mary Jo."

Billy Ray tried to hold back the tears but could not control them. The tears have a mind of their own. As fast as he wiped his eyes, the more the tears continued to run down his face. Mary Jo bent down and put her arms around his neck in comfort, letting him know she understood. Billy Ray knew his mama was going to be happy when she got the dresses. Looking at Mary Jo, Billy Ray thanked her for such a good deed.

By this time, the twins saw what Mary Jo had done and they started crying too. B. J. was so deep in a science book that he had found that he missed it. Mary Jo quickly had to take charge of the saturation before everyone started balling. "Hey, hey!" Mary Jo said, "There are still other places we haven't checked out."

The gang was happy now as they went to find more treasures. "Maybe if we are careful we might find some money too," Mary Jo said. They now realized there were lot of places they needed to go too. Mary Jo had everyone put their treasures in the wagon. Billy Ray got up, wiping his hand across his tear-stained face. He put the dresses back in the bag and laid them in the back of the wagon. You could hear the gang's happy voices walking up the alley to someone else's house. Coming up with a good idea, Billy Ray said, "We can find some money and buy a dime's worth of wieners and a pack of marshmallows. We can have a wiener roast later on, huh? huh? huh? Mary Jo?"

Everybody started getting excited about the wiener roast, even Mary Jo agreed with the gang that would be nice for the twins. Billy Ray was happy and started looking for pop bottles to sell. Along with the rest of the gang, they searched through those big barrels. They found some pennies and four Coca-Cola bottles to sell at Mr. Young's store. Now they knew this was the best alley hunt yet. The twins had their heads down in the big can, mumbling about all of the stuff they found.

Mary Jo definitely needed to look over the stuff the twins had collected. She decided that they should not take any of the treasures home with them. Their mama would have a fit knowing they were down in those nasty alleys. The twins' daddy being a doctor too.
Just the thought made Mary Jo tell the twins to leave their stuff at the playhouse. The twins agreed to Mary Jo's suggestion and continued to look for more treasures. This was the best day and the gang had fun.

Simple Pleasures

CHAPTER XXXIII
DINNER FOR THE TWINS

After a while, Mary Jo thought about the big surprise she was having for the gang. Billy Ray was really enjoying himself after finding some more pop bottles. He didn't have time to be emotional anymore. The gang let Mary Jo know that this was a good plan for the day. This was the best day for the alley hunt. It was not raining. It was just right to walk in the alleys.

"Gosh lee! Mary Jo," Billy Ray said. "This was the greatest day ever, huh, gang?" The twins were concerned about what Billy Ray was saying and stared at him but didn't ask any questions. This was the wrong thing Billy Ray could have said to Mary Jo. She already thought that she was as bright as the teacher. What he said would surely make her head swell even bigger.

Mary Jo, very conceited, said, "Oh! It wasn't that hard trying to think of something for us to do today, Billy Ray. I was walking and the idea just came to me. I do say it was such a great idea to go alley hunting."

She went on to tell them that she could not sleep because she wanted the day to be exciting. It had to be something that would be adventurous. Having fun, searching for that hidden treasures that could bring joy to the gang. We had to have a good time today. Mary Jo told them the idea about going alley hunting just came out of the blue. It was one of the good things that the gang would get so hyped up doing. They heard all of her fanfare now but did not realize what she had said earlier. When she was waving her hands and throwing up her head like she was starring in one of those musicals. She proudly told the gang, "Oh! It was not hard trying to think of something."

B. J. stared at Billy Ray with a look and pointed his hand towards Mary Jo with a disapproving gesture. Now just look at her he thought. Once you get this girl started it's like winding a clock up. B. J. was very peeved and had enough of her acting as he said, "Let's go, gang."

Mary Jo easily without any trouble came to her senses. She noticed that the gang was no longer interested in her performance. They had enough of her acting and walked away from her. She had to run to catch up with them. B. J. looked at her running and just shook his head. The twins were tired of Mary Jo and her acting too. They showed it by not asking her what she was doing.

It was getting late and the gang decided this was enough alley hunting for today. B. J. put his science books with all of the other things he had collected while Billy Ray was slowly pulling the wagon. B. J. wished that he could have "found some bugs." Mary Jo heard him mumbling something. He really did not go in for all that other junk that the gang found.

Looking over at B. J., Mary Jo could not believe what her ears just heard. This boy was actually standing there bothering the good Lord for his bugs. She called out to B. J. "Stop and hush your fuss." She told him that, "The good Lord, under no circumstance, want to hear his weird prayer.

Mary Jo was serious and wanted B. J. to hear her. She let B. J. know that the Lord would send a big streak of lightning down here. She was into it now with her hands on those two bones again and reminding B. J. of the hundred million bugs in his room already. "So just stop it."

"You don't know a thing about the Bible Mary Jo," B. J. arrogantly said.

One could wonder where Mary Jo was getting her information on knowing so much about the Bible. She acted as if she read the word every day and night during the week and three times on Sunday. Mary Jo smarty remind B. J. what Hezekiah said in the "Bible?" Poor boy did not realize that Hezekiah is not a book, it is someone's name. He began to rub his hand across his face and questioned himself, but did remember the time she did give him a good answer to the question about girls. Mary Jo was very perturbed and stood waiting for an answer. He thought that he better leave it alone and agree with her. "Yeah, Mary Jo, you are right."

Billy Ray wanted to go before it got too late. He had enough of Mary Jo and B. J. 's lesson on the Bible. They need to go to Mr. Young's store to get the stuff for the wiener roast. Along with being a little in need of some food, Billy Ray was ready to go. They all decided to go shouting "A wiener roast for the twins."

Mr. Young's store was just down the hill from Mary Jo's house. It was on Main Street. The gang decided to drop off their junk at the playhouse and then go to the store. Miss Clean, Mary Jo wanted the gang to wash their hands under the faucet outside the house. Her mama always kept a bar of lye soap on the windowsill. This was for Mary Jo to wash her hands before she came into the house. As the gang washed their hands, the smell of food was lingering in the air.

Billy Ray was the first to say, "hum, hum, that shore smells good. What your mama cooking Mary Jo?"

"Now let me see," playing with how she would answer. Mary Jo said as she put her hand under her chin. Talking with her deep southern accent she said, "It's just some old golden fried chicken with brown gravy on the side, corn on the cob, greens, candied yams, a blackberry cobbler, and some hot water cornbread."

"Shut your mouth girl," Billy Ray howled. "You know we are hungry."

Little did they know that the dinner was for them? Mary Jo asked her mama several days ago if she would fix a going away dinner for the twins. Mrs. Finney put her hands on her hips and said, "Mary Jo, baby, that's a good deed yoes wonts to do."

You can bet that is where Mary Jo gets putting her hands on her hips from, her mama. She had kept it to herself until now. Mary Jo proudly let the gang know that, "The dinner is for you all and a going away present for the twins."

Their little eyes sparkled in the twilight with delight. The gang was happy as they all gathered around Mary Jo. Another proud moment for their leader. The gang shouted. "Yeah!"

All you could hear was, "Mm mm, smell that food."

The aroma lingered in the air as the little gang sniffed every breath they took. Mary Jo had her nose in the air as if she could taste the smell of food. "Oh! Gosh lee," she said. She continued, "The musters and collard greens with a little vinegar and that hot water cornbread that my mama cooked is goin to be eatin by these fingers. I'm going to crumble that cornbread up in them greens and eat them with my fingers."

Billy Ray said, "Oh shucks, Mary Jo. You would make a cow want some of them greens."

Mary Jo, shaking her head, said, "I know because they are that good."

In the meantime, Mrs. Finney came to the kitchen door. She held the screen door open and motioned for the gang to come in, "If its hands were washed."
Billy Ray, nodding his head, led the pack into the kitchen. My, my, the twins were thinking as they looked at all that food on the table. Billy Ray was walking fast and smacking his lips as he rubbed his hands together.

Mrs. Finney got the kids attention and blessed the food. They all sat down to a big feast. B. J. felt as if he was about to starve as he reached for his plate. Hurriedly, put food in his mouth, B. J. savored the favor. Mrs. Finney laughed and enjoyed the moment the kids eating as if this was their last meal. There would be plenty more for them to eat if they wanted it. Mary Jo was deep in her eating those greens, no matter how many times her mama cooked greens Mary Jo just love eating them.

Billy Ray had butter from the sweet yellow corn dripping down his fingers. And yes, Mary Jo did just like she said, using her fingers to mix her cornbread in her greens. You could hear her say, "UN, un, uh," as she popped the greens and cornbread in her mouth.

The twins were too busy eating crispy fried chicken that made you lick your fingers. The thought crossed B. J.'s mind to thank Mary Jo. Indeed, this was such a lovely day. The dinner that she planned just topped off everything. However, being smart as he was B. J. just tapped his foot; He thought, she knows.

Mrs. Finney looked at the children and shook her head saying, "Take yoes time heah. There is plenty more fore yoe."

She decided to let the children eat in peace and walked to the living room. "Boy! Oh, Boy Mary Jo," the gang said, "You really done it this time. We had a good time all day today and especially now."

"Wow! What a time we had," Billy Ray said. He licked his fingers getting the butter off them. The gang wanted to save some room in their stomachs for that blackberry cobbler. Every now and then one of them would get up from the table, go over to the stove and look at the golden-brown crust. You could see the juice seeping up through the crust. Then all you could hear were the snacking of their lips. They were enjoying their food to the very last bite.

Billy Ray decided that the gang needed to give Mary Jo three cheers for her great plans for today. The gang all stood up and said, "Three cheers for Mary Jo."

Mary Jo was really going to be something now. She smiled showing all of her little teeth. "Rah, rah, rah!" The gang shouted as loud as they could.

Mrs. Finney laughed when she heard them giving Mary Jo some cheers. They couldn't believe that Mary Jo didn't get on her soapbox. She seemed to be speechless as they continued to cheer her. After the cheers, the gang tried to make room for that blackberry cobbler. That did not work. Mrs. Finney's dinner was so filling that the gang had to wait until tomorrow for the cobbler. They all made a promise that they would be back as soon as it was daylight.

After a while, Mrs. Finney came back into the kitchen. The gang was rubbing their stomachs and thanking Mary Jo again for a good day. Mrs. Finney guessed that the gang could not eat any of her cobber tonight. She suggested that they could come back, "Tomorrow afternoon" echoed throughout the kitchen. They were serious about that cobbler and the next afternoon was too late. Mrs. Finney jokingly asked, "Oh, is dat too early?"

She knew that they wanted to be there first thing in the morning. She said, "All rite. Come back when your mamas tells yoes too."

They agreed to come back in the morning. The boys left and took the twins' home. Mary Jo could not remember when she had such a great time. She said, "It was fun having some friends to share these summer days with. The twins and the boys look to me to plan fun things for them to do. I know now that I am indeed the one to make this summer a time we will not forget. It's a world to be discovered beside B. J.'s bugs, the twins' twenty questions, and Billy Ray's airplanes. They will be able to explore, find, do, and enjoy the simple pleasures that summer has to offer."

CHAPTER XXXIV
CHASING A RAINBOW

It's been almost two weeks since the twins left on their vacation and things around the playhouse just was not the same. Mary Jo had nothing to do around the house but stare out into space. Mrs. Finney would see her moping around with her head drooping. She is her mother and this almost broke her heart. She knew that her baby was lonely and it was even harder, having no sister or brother to play with. "She needs to find someum exciting that would bes fun," Mrs. Finney said

Mrs. Finney stood with her hand under her chin pondering what would be good for Mary Jo to do. Then she remembered something she had in the attic. She quickly went upstairs and as she walked across the room, her footsteps made an echoing sound on the wooden floor. Her mind was on getting into that steamer trunk sitting next to a straw bottom rocking chair. Opening up the big lid slowly to not disturb whatever was in the trunk, she lifted the tray out and set it on the floor. In the bottom of the trunk was a tattered brown bag. She carefully took the bag out and laid it gently on the floor. The thought of what the bag held began to bring memories. Her eyes were stinging from the dust as she took out a quilt made from feed sacks, gunny sacks, flour sacks, and potato sacks.

It's painstakingly sewn by hand, with cotton thread, and tied with colorful strings of yarn. In the middle of this rare pattern was a wrench. This represented freedom. Mrs. Finney thought as she slowly looked around the room that it had been a while since she had been up in the attic and cobwebs and dust were everywhere. She searched around until she found a straw broom over near the little window in the corner. She began to sweep the dust and knock the cobwebs down with her broom. Using a little mother's wit, Mrs. Finney began to sing one of those church songs. She was hoping that Mary Jo would hear her and come up.

She got her wish because Mary Jo, being inquisitive, wanted to know why her mama was so happy. She wondered what was going on. Climbing two stairs at a time, she was up the long flight of stairs quickly. Mary Jo could hear her mama really singing like she was at church.

Simple Pleasures

Mary Jo stood breathless in the doorway looking at her mama sweeping and singing. Mrs. Finney pretend she did not see her and continued sweeping. Mary Jo was agitated as she said, "Mama, what in the world are you doing?"

"Mindin my business child. What have yoes ben doin?"

"Oh nothing, mama-just standing on the porch looking down the road being lonely," she said.

The scent from the mothballs lingered in the air as she thought. "They are up here, too. huh?"

Mrs. Finney humming her song came over to Mary Jo and held her face in her hands. Then she said in her motherly way, "I've got something fore yoes baby."

Mary Jo's little eyes were bright like a sparkle on the Fourth of July. She could not wait to see what her mama had to show her. This was the hi-lite of her day. "What is it mama, what is it?"

"Oh, hush yoes fuss child and wait."

She took her by the hand and led her over to sit on an old apple crate. Mary Jo, like a little kid, hastily sat down and watched her mama. She was still anxiously wanting to know where the big surprise was.? She scanned the room like having x-ray vision for a clue but did not see anything. It is hot and dusty up there and her mama did not make matters any better by sweeping. Mrs. Finney knew how impatient Mary Jo could be, and quickly walked across the floor to the old trunk again. She took out the tattered patch-quilt and walked at a fast pace back across the floor. Mary Jo quietly waited as she sat looking wide-eyed and wondering what her mama was doing. Her mama walked over to where Mary Jo was sitting and held out the quilt. Mrs. Finney looked at the quilt with great pride letting Mary Jo know it know it's history.

The quilt belonged to her great-great-grand grandma and Mary Jo noticed the condition the quilt was in. Mary Jo was wondering why didn't great-great-grandma just go to the store and buy her a quilt? The department stores sale a variety of blankets and patchwork quilt.

Mrs. Finney felt that Mary Jo would ask her about buying a quilt and miss the importance of knowing what her great-great-grandma's quilt meant. She knew that the quilt she held in her hand meant freedom. Sorrowfully, saying she let Mary Jo know, "They couldn't go to noes store and buy things like wes can today. Deys weres slaves and worked fore their masters."

Her mama gently laid the quilt across Mary Jo's arms as the smell of mothballs filled her noses. Mary Jo didn't want her mama to think that she was not interested in what she was telling her. The smell of the mothballs was too much, but for her mama's sake she continued to listen to the story and held on to every word. Mary Jo realized that her ancestors were slaves and did not get paid for their labor.

    She went on to tell her how her great-great-grandma would have to work from before the sun came up until late in the evening seven days a week. When the children were older like her, they had to work hard in the fields too.

    Mary Jo interrupted her mama wanting to know where she got all her information. "Who told you that story?"

    Her mama smiled and continued telling Mary Jo that her grandma told them. They would all sit around the fireplace at night and her grandmother would tell the children this many years ago. "Yoes see dis hean quilt yore great-great-grandma would takes de emptie flour sacks, potatter sacks, feed sacks, and gunny sacks and makes thees things dey need."

    This got Mary Jo's attention as she wondered about their clothes. Her mama tenderly looked at Mary Jo and told her they made everything. Her mom continued to give her daughter a history lesson about her ancestors.

    She picked up the quilt and proudly held it up so Mary Jo could see it. Mrs. Finney had Mary Jo's complete attention as she explained the meaning of the quit. She pointed to the quilt and told her it was a freedom quilt, "see, the wrench in each square? Dey was known as the working tools. My grandma's mama was one of those people who got away and went up north."

    Mary Jo was on the edge of the crate as she waited to hear more of her mama's story. She began to imagine she was there with her mama, sitting around the fireplace, listening to her great-grandmother. The cracking of the fire, the glow from the candles illuminated the room. Mrs. Finney continued to capture Mary Jo's mind with the story of the past.

    You could see how Mary Jo was in deep thought as she could hear the words her mama softy singing 'goina to chase me rainbow tonight,' "de slaves would know it was the right time to run away dat night. Yoes see de slaves wasn't posed to talk to each other when dey work. Des use all kinds of signs with their hands and drawing pictures on de ground. De headmaster wouldn't noes what dey was doing. Some had created a language they called pig Latin saying the word backwards and adding the letter A."

    Still full of questions, Mary Jo wanted to know, "How did they know the secret word, if they wasn't allowed to talk to each other?"

Mrs. Finney looked at Mary Jo with a tear in her eye and said, "Baby thees would sing. Dey would make up song and de secret words would bees in de song."

"Wow!" she anxiously said. "Mama that was pretty smart of my great-great-grandma, huh?"

Mary Jo learned that was how her great-great-grandma got away. Somebody was singin "goina 'chase me a rainbow tonight' and hang de wrench pattern quilt on de line before dark." This captured Mary Jo's attention; she was amazed at what she learned in the attic.

Her mama's eyes begin to tear up even more and Mary Jo gently put her little hands around her mama's neck. They stayed embraced like that for a while. Her mama continued to cry softly. Mary Jo was proud of the story her mama shared with her. Mrs. Finney lifted her apron to her face and wiped the tears away. She looked at Mary Jo and was glad to have a child like her. Mrs. Finney laughed and gave Mary Jo a big kiss.

CHAPTER XXXV
MAKING A QUILT

Mrs. Finney took Mary Jo's little hand and they walked over to search out the old trunk. It was like hunting for treasures. The old trunk held a lot of old things her mama had saved. Mrs. Finney took out a quilt her mama made for her before she died. Maybe, someday it might belong to Mary Jo. It had the wedding ring pattern with two gold bands interlocking each other and made from different colors of satin.

"You think I will get it when I get married?" Mary Jo asked her mama.

Mrs. Finney began to tease her saying, "Noe body goina get my baby."

"Mama, not right now," she said. "Maybe when I am nineteen."

They laughed and her mama picked up the bag and decided to let Mary Jo make a quilt. She was so overjoyed about making a quilt, Mary Jo began to jump up and down and being a kid that got her joy back. Her mama began to take the bag with the cloth in it to show her how to match them. The cut pieces of material put together would make a lovely quilt. Mary Jo was excited that she finally had something to do. They gathered up the quilt pieces and headed downstairs. Forgetting as usual, Mary Jo jumped the stairs two at a time. She heard a loud "No!" coming out of her mama's mouth. Immediately, Mary Jo knew what the "no" meant.

Many times her mama told Mary Jo not to jump the stairs two at a time. She was only trying to protect Mary Jo from falling down the stairs and hurting herself. "The stairs are for you to walk up or down them and not play on them." She instructed.

Distracting her Mama and her rules, Mary Jo put her arm around her waist. She took her mama's hand and went in the kitchen to do their work on the table. The noonday sun was shining brightly through the kitchen window making it hotter. Mrs. Finney picked up her paper fan from the table and began to fan herself. "Woo! It's getting hotter by dee hour, huh child?" Mary Jo, looking unconcerned, was excited about making her own quilt, responded, "Uh hun."

"I's noes," her mama said as an idea popped into her mind. She walked across the floor thinking about the cold jar of Kool-Aid in the icebox. "This will help, huh baby?" She said.

Simple Pleasures

Mary Jo, still anxious, wanted some of the biscuits left over from the morning. The jar of blackberry jam was still setting on the table. Mrs. Finney already knew that Mary Jo might be getting hungry so she walked over to the stove and took out the pan of biscuits from the warmer. She was saving the biscuits for a bread pudding she was going to make later.

Her mama gave Mary Jo a big smile as she put the pan of biscuits on the table. Mary Jo picked up the still warm biscuit and spread butter and jelly on it. You could hear, "OOOOOH!" sound as she munched on the biscuit with blackberry jam.

While Mary Jo was busy eating her biscuits, her mama decided she would lay the pieces of cut pattern out on the table. Then they could match each piece and sew it together. The colored yarn, the silver thimble, cotton thread, and the basting needle were neatly placed next to her scissors. These were all the things she would need to make a quilt.

Then she pulled a chair closer to Mary Jo and told her to watch. Mary Jo could hardly wait as excitement rose up in her. Her eyes were on every move that her mama made and what she did with the piece of pattern in her hand. She was excited and happy now that her mama had told her some history about her family. Mary Jo was enjoying her snack and the time she was spending with her mama. Her spirit was lifted as she continued to watch her mama.

Mary Jo hurriedly finished her snack. She knew her mama would want her to wash her hands first. Mary Jo jumped up from the table and went over to the sink to wash her hands. Mrs. Finney, smiling, thought, I's didn't have to tell her. She watched Mary Jo as she did a little tap dance across the kitchen floor. Her mama laughed as she said, "Girl, yoes shore is funny."

How happy her mama was as she noticed that her baby wasn't lonely anymore. She began to sing a song again. Mary Jo was wondering why her mama didn't go in the big time. She heard of other singers really making it big in show business. Feeling a little nervous about asking her mama such a grown-up question, Mary Jo abruptly said, "Mama, how come you never sung for some of those big bands? You have such a pretty voice."

Her mama, was a little bit taken back by the question but said, "Oh! baby, dis voice of mine ain't dat good is it?"

Taking her mama's hand she said, "Mama, you sing like a lark that wakes us up in the morning."

"Well!" her mama excitedly said. "De good Lord gave me dis voice and I's just sing for him."

Softly Mary Jo said, "Sure mama," as she gave her a big hug.

CHAPTER XXXVI
A SURPRISE VISIT FROM B.J.

B. J. was making his way up to the backdoor step howling, "Mary Jo, Mary Jo, come on out!" Quickly getting up from the table, she ran across the wooden floor to the backdoor and was surprised to see B. J.

Finally seeing some of the gang, Mary Jo was happy and invited B. J. to come in. B. J. hopped up the steps and hastily walked into the kitchen saying, "Oh, hello Mrs. Finney," then politely said, "How are you doing today?"

"Sonny boy," she happily said "I's fine, just fine. And how de family?"

B. J. wondered why grown-ups always want to know about the family, especially since they see them at church? Huh, it just beat everything. Immersed in his thoughts he finally said, "They are just fine, fine," as he shook his head.

He really didn't want to talk with Mrs. Finney, after all, he didn't know what to talk to her about. He looked in Mary Jo's direction looking for some help. He came to see her, not to hold a conversation with her mama.

Mrs. Finney sensed that B.J. didn't want to her talk anymore and quietly excused herself and she left the kids alone to enjoy themselves. She left the kitchen and walked down the hall. Then she remembered that she still had to show Mary Jo how to sew the pattern.

Mary Jo sat patiently waiting to make a great quilt like her ancestors. She wanted to give her children a quilt someday too. A smile was on her face as the excitement and anticipation rose up in her. It didn't matter to her that B. J. was there. This was her time of happiness and doing things with her mama. She must have been concentrating too hard because she was calling her mama.

Mrs. Finney abruptly said, "What de matter, for yoes child?"

"Oh! Uh, what about making the quilt?" Maybe B. J. would like to help?" She asked. Looking puzzled, B. J. just stared and asked, "What quilt?"

"B. J., my mama is helping me make a quilt. You see all the patterns on the table?" Mary Jo said, sounding frustrated with the question he was asking.

Simple Pleasures

"Yeah! That's nice," he said as he pulled out a chair to sit down. Mrs. Finney began to show Mary Jo and B. J. what they had to do first.

"Hean what yoes do first," Mrs. Finney said as she picked up the needle and began to thread it. Mary Jo and B. J. looked on with anticipation. They were ready to start sewing. Mrs. Finney took two pieces of the pattern and begin to sew them together. She slowly sewed the pattern together so that Mary Jo could see how it was done.

"Now take yore needle, Mary Jo and B. J., and thread them," her mama said. Then she took them through each step of sewing the two patterns together.

B. J. hurriedly sewed his two pieces together and proudly showed Mary Jo how easily it is done. Mary Jo didn't want to be outdone. She tried sewing her two pieces of material together. B. J. looked at Mary Jo's pieces and began to laugh. "My sewing is better than yours, Mary Jo."

Laughing she said, "Boys don't know how to sew better than girls huh, mama?" Mrs. Finney didn't want to get in their petty conversation. She looked at Mary Jo and said, "I's not goin to git in dat mess with you and B. J."

However, she said, "I's will say dis, dat most women's clothes are made by men tailors." This hit a sour note with Mary Jo. She felt that her mama was taking sides with B. J. She never heard that men made all of women's clothes. Mary Jo wondered, if her mama just wanted B. J. to feel good hum. "Oh! Oh, oh," Mary Jo said, as if something was really hurting her. "Mama! You shouldn't have told B. J. that. Now his head is really going to be too big for his good."

"Ha, ha, ha," B. J. said as he finished his piece of work first. He thought, wow, this is fun and now I finally can do something better than she can.

"Ah, B. J., my mama has a quilt my great-great-grandma made," Mary Jo proudly said trying to get B. J.'s mind off what her mama had just said.

"Can I see it? Please let me see it!" B. J. exclaimed. Putting her hand across her mouth, Mary Jo thought, oh boy, I know I've started something now. He might try to see if he could discover some dead bug on the quilt.

B. J., guessing what Mary Jo must be thinking, said, "I'm not going to search for any bugs," as a frown crossed his face.

Mrs. Finney thought it's time for her to get out of their mess and go outside and hoe in her garden. Thess chillin needs to be alone now.

"I's goin to hoe in my garden," she said as she went over to the stove to get some ashes to put on her plants.

"Mama's bugs still trying to eat up your plants again?" Mary Jo said, looking concerned.

"Yeah! Child, dey has to eat too, I's guess. Dat's why I's was gitting these here ashes to sprinkle on the plants. That'll kill dem vermin off for shore, uh, huh, shore will. Well! I's would leave yoes chillin to yoes selves." She went out the door into the backyard to her garden.

Mary Jo continued to sew her cut patterns together, thinking how nice it was going to look when she finished. B. J. said, "Hey Mary Jo, it never crossed my mind how much work it took to make a quilt."

"Yeah! Huh, B. J., it a lot of work."

"Yep, you bet, Mary Jo, this is work," B. J. replied. "I never realized how much work it is making a quilt. We just get under it when we go to bed and not think somebody had to make it. We just get into bed and cover up huh, Mary Jo?"

Well, this was a great day for the two of them. Mary Jo learned that her great-great-grandma was one of the slaves who chased a rainbow and found freedom at the end of it. Even though B. J. didn't get to hear the whole story, he got to share in the art of making a quilt.

"Just think B. J.," Mary Jo said, "I'm the fifth generation to make a quilt that's nice."

However, B.J. was in his own little world. He wasn't paying too much attention to her. This didn't sit too well with Mary Jo. She was very irritated by B. J. not answering her. She really let him have it as she said, "Don't you dare sit over there like you don't hear me!"

"Oh! Yeah, that's nice," B. J. said.

"Why didn't you answer me B. J.?" she angrily asked.

"I'm sorry. I was just thinking about what you said about your great-great- grandma, that's all," B. J. responded.

B. J. was wondering who helped them get away. He really wanted to know as he got up enough nerve to ask her. This was a no-no as Mary Jo went into one of her performances. Standing up from her chair, she said saying in a sassy way, "I don't know. Why do you want to know? I wasn't there to know, B. J. There you go, trying to get into other folks' business. You just too nosy." B. J. figured he better not get into any deep discussion with this girl. She probably would tell him that "the Lord said it."

Time seemed to pass so quickly. B. J. realized that it was time to go home. Mrs. Finney was coming through the door as he was saying goodbye. He asked if it was all right to come back tomorrow. Mrs. Finney chuckled as she said, "Shore child, come on back. Mary Jo be glad for yoes to come."

Since the twins had been gone, she really didn't have anyone to play with. Mrs. Finney continued getting her bread ready to make a bread pudding.

"B.J., if you promise not to bother me with threading needle, you can come back tomorrow" Mary Jo said.

B. J. replied that he could thread his own needle and sew better than she could. His voice trailed off as he said, "I will see you tomorrow and I will make my whole quilt tomorrow." He laughed and went down the steps headed up the path.

"Hurry home, sonny boy, so yoe mama won't be worryin hean," Ms. Finney demanded.

"Yes ma'am," B. J. replied.

Mrs. Finney was so happy that her baby had a good day. She went over to the table and gingerly patted Mary Jo on the head. Mary Jo gave her mama a big smile and said, "Thank you, Mama. This was so much fun."

"Well, baby, yoes better git dat stuff off the table now so I's could finish cooking de supper."

Mary Jo joyfully began to pick up all her little patterns she sewed together. Eagerly and proudly, she showed her mama how many squares she sewed together.

"Uh hum! Child, dat's gonna be some kind of quilt," her mama said.

Mary Jo laughed really thinking that she was making a pretty quilt. Her mama really didn't want to make Mary Jo feel bad. Mrs. Finney knew Mary Jo had sewn the pieces of material together on the wrong side. They had uneven pieces. It was a mess, Mrs. thought as she shook her head. "However, I's guess Mary Jo did do her best."

She smiled and walked over to the stove. It would soon be time for supper and she need to check on her food. Mrs. Finney took the poker off the hook beside the stove and stirred up the fire. She had greens and black-eyed peas that were cooking on the back of the stove.

"Hum-hum-mm." Dey are nearly done, just a little more cooking," she said.

In the meantime, Mary Jo finished putting away the cut-up quilt patterns and came back into the kitchen. She walked across the floor over near the stove where her mama was stirring her food.

"Mama!" she happily said. "I really like making the quilt and learning about my great-great-grandma." Mary Jo gently put her hand around her mama's waist and said, "Mama, I love you. This day was the best."

As Mary Jo looked up at her mama, she was happy that she wasn't lonely anymore. She had fun just playing with her mama and B. J. Mary Jo thought, I didn't know that an old woman like my mama could be so much fun.

Mrs. Finney sensed that her baby was finally happy, and this really was a fun day. She smiled, thinking I's can't let Mary Jo noes B.J. can sew better than she can. Hun shore can. But if Mary Jo keep on trying, she git good at it one of dees days. Mrs. Finney finished cooking and Mary Jo sat at the table very happy.

Simple Pleasures

CHAPTER XXXVII
THE PICNIC

It is summer and everyone in the little town of Johnson City, Tennessee, is fighting off those pesky mosquitoes. The month of July seemed to be when the mosquitoes were so worrisome. However, the townspeople had a remedy for the pest. They would get themselves old rags, wet it just a bit and then light it. The smoke from the old rag would drive those mosquitoes away.

Most folks liked to come over to sit and gossip with Mrs. Finney. Her porch was built like Dr. Johnson's porch that went around both sides of the house. Mary Jo's mama enjoyed sitting on the porch in the cool of the evening. The women especially liked to come over and sit in the straw chairs for hours talking about their men, the war, and how good their gardens were growing. Maybe a little town gossip would find its way into their conversations with a few giggles afterward. Then one of the ladies would say, "Honey yoes better shut yoes mouth, cause yoe noes it dee truth." Then the giggles would start as one of the women would get up with her hands on her hips mocking whomever they were talking about.

In the meantime, Mary Jo and her friends would be playing hide-and-seek, ring-around-the-rosy, tag, or acting out one of their favorite cowboys and Indian's movies. These are the times and days that Mary Jo and her friends would remember when they were grown. This is the important part of being a kid in the summer.

Then there is the Fourth of July parade down Main Street. This would be a big treat, as the town's folk would celebrate America's birthday. The old-timers who fought in World War I would march down the street with their badges, banners, and medals. They would be gaily waving their hands as they passed by the crowd. Some of the old-timers would only have parts of their uniforms on. Maybe they would only have the jacket on because time had stretched their body and their pants were too tight or too small to wear anymore. However, that didn't matter to them. They were proud to have fought for such a great and grand old country.

The colored folk would line the curbs to watch their little band and their five majorettes would put on a show. The lead majorette was a fair-skinned colored girl with long slender legs like any fine prancing horse. She would march with her legs stepping high. Then she would make a turn, and toss her baton in the air and catch it as she turned back around. The people would shout and cheer. In that moment Mrs. Finney would proudly say, "That's my girl!"

Mary Jo would look up at her mama and say, "Mama, that's what I'm going to be." Her mama would proudly say, "That's good, my child."

After the parade was over, Mrs. Finney and Mary Jo, along with some other folks would pile upon Mr. Henry's flatbed truck. There would be plenty of hay spread out on the truck. Mr. Henry sold watermelons, bushels of peaches, snap green beans, apples, and some of the sweetest cantaloupes this side of the Mississippi. The hay would keep the watermelons cool and from moving all over the place.

Everybody in the little town were going over to Placerville, to the county fair. That was the place to be, to have a picnic, to enjoy the rides, the "blue ribbon" winners, and to watch the fireworks later on that night. You could hear those old women with their hands on their hips telling the men to be careful how they handled the big baskets filled with fried chicken, barbecue ribs, sweet yellow corn on the cob, potato salad, baked beans, and those delicious pound cakes that Mrs. Finney made.

Old toothless Slim would be in the way saying, "Now, now! Yoes knows Mrs. Finney done gone and put her foot in dat there cakes." Then he would burst out with one of his belly laughs.

"Oh, hush yoes fuss, Slim," Mrs. Finney would say. "I's knows what yoes up to and yoes better wait till wes git to Placerville. Aint no uses of yoes gitting yoes mouth ready."
"Go on!" one of the men would say to old man Slim. "Git on up on the truck. Yoes in the way, now git."

Old toothless Slim would slide along as one of the men helped him upon the truck. Mary Jo and B. J. would be playing in the hay until one of the grown-ups would make them stop and sit still. She would say something smart under her breath as she smiled and said, "Yes ma'am."

Finally, everything was ready to go. Mr. Henry would take off down the road to Placerville. Mrs. would start singing and everybody would join in. The fun would begin as old toothless Slim would try to sing along. Someone would say, "Oh, hush your fuss, Slim. Yoes sound like a dying calf in a hailstorm."

Simple Pleasures

Old Slim would say, "In my day I could out sing all of yoes young snappers."

"When was dat Slim in 1919?" one of his friends would say, joking.

Everybody would burst out laughing.

"Now yoes just leave Slim alone now," Mrs. Finney would say. "Yoes just jealous, UN hun! jealous," as she began to sing again and clapping her hands. Old Slim began to do his "ham bone" to the beat of the song. His long thin hands would sound out a beat on his legs as he would pop his lip to the song. In the meantime, B. J. and Mary Jo would be listening to everything the grown-ups would say so they could talk about it later. Mary Jo would be the main one to act out what everybody said. She had them all figured out except her mama. She would say, "God would strike me dead for mocking mt mama."

B. J., looking puzzled, said "For truth Mary Jo?"

"Yeah! And I am not going to do it neither, so don't keep asking me." She said.

Changing the subject, she asked, "What are you going to ride first at the fair, B. J.?"

"Wow! Oh, let me see, I haven't really thought about it," he said. B. J. finally decided on riding the Ferris wheel first. "It will take you up where the sky is blue and the sun is shining hot on your face." He responded

"Yeah!" he said, the sound of excitement in his voice. That's what I am going to ride, he was thinking. Un huh. He leaned back in the hay and put a piece of straw in the corner of his mouth.

Mary Jo noticed how B. J. was getting to be a nice-looking kid. Hum, she thought. I wonder if I have changed this summer, too. Mary Jo began to inspect herself but was disappointed, thinking the bumps haven't gotten any bigger, my legs are still the same and my hips are still the same. Nothing has changed.

B. J. noticed the strange look on Mary Jo's face and asked, "What are you looking for?" Mary Jo was too embarrassed to let B. J. know what she was looking at. What was going on in that brain of hers?

"Oh nothing, B. J. nothing," Mary Jo quickly said as she leaned up looking at B. J. They started talking again and wondering where Billy Ray was. Mary Jo hadn't seen him since the big dinner for the twins. B. J. agreed with Mary Jo about the last time Billy Ray was around. It was definitely the last time they all went alley hunting. "Where is Billy Ray?" B.J. asked.

"How come no one has seen him?" Mary Jo excitedly said, "You know, B. J., I haven't seen Billy Ray at all."

Mary Jo's little brain began to come up with all kinds of crazy thoughts. B. J. anxiously said, "That was the last time I saw him, too. Maybe, we will see him at the fair."

Mary Jo whispered, "You know that's the only time his daddy takes him anywhere."

"Shore is!" B. J. shouted out and quickly looked around to see if the grown folks noticed him. He suddenly realized that Mary Jo had told him something everybody else already knew. This was the usual thing that Billy Ray's daddy did every year.

As soon as they setup under that big oak tree near the creek they decided to go looking for Billy Ray. They both realized that they missed Billy Ray being around. It was during this moment that it hit them like a bolt of lightning.

Finally, B. J. let Mary Jo know how he felt. He shyly said, "I sort of miss Billy Ray along with the twins. We really had a good time so far this summer." However, Mary Jo was thinking about the good time she had with B. J. over at her house. Now he was talking about missing the twins and Billy Ray. Stunned by what B. J. just said. Mary Jo rudely reminded him that they made a quilt.

"That would have been more fun if the whole gang were there," B.J. said.

"It was alright, but it just wasn't the same."

Feeling a little rejected, Mary Jo knew that she wasn't going to win this time. She lay back in the hay and looked up at the sky. She noticed one cloud that looked like a dog and said, "Wow! Look at that cloud with the face like a dog."

"Gosh, lee, Mary Jo, it shore does," B.J. said.

However, Mary Jo decided not to bother him and got lost in her thoughts. It seemed like it took no time at all to get to the fairgrounds. She leaned up from the hay and noticed the big truck pulling-up to a parking space. Everybody began to jump off the truck. In the meantime, the women started giving orders like a Sergeant. Mrs. Finney seemed to be the leader. She told the men folk to get the heavy things off first, then carry them over by the big tree where old man Sam is waiting.

Trying to get out of taking anything over to the picnic area, B. J. and Mary Jo tried to sneak off. They hid behind the big sign that was near the entrance, but Mrs. Finney had eyes like an eagle. Putting hands on her hips she said loudly, "Mary Jo and sonny boy! Yose just march yoeself right back hean. Yore all grab some of dis food. Yoes nos yoes bees de first to wont somein to eat."

Mary Jo had her lips sticking out so far that someone could have come along and walked on them. However, when she got close to where her mama was standing, she had a smile on her face. Mrs. Finney was standing and tapping her foot.

"Mary Jo Ruth Finney," her mama called out, "Yoes git yoeself right over here. You go to dat truck and carry some of dem boxes with the three apple pies in it. Yoes hean?"

Simple Pleasures

Mary Jo was really hot under the collar by now as she said, "Yes ma'am, mama." She briskly walked over to the truck talking to herself. "Why I got to carry anything? Did I help put this stuff on this old truck? What is mama doing just giving everybody orders? She is acting like she was in the army?" Right, then, and there, Mary Jo decided that when she grows up, her children wouldn't have to do nothing. Breaking into her thoughts her mama called out, "What's taking yoes so long? Git a move on, yoes girl."

She, was some kind of mad by now but what could a kid do? Mary Jo thought. She muttered, "Mama, you should have come and got your own pies, huh!"

Nevertheless, Mary Jo answered aloud, saying, "I'm coming mama."

"Yoes just slow yoreself down fore yoes drop dem pies youngin," her mama said. Mary Jo was really perturbed as she carefully carried the three pies over to the table. She set the precious pies down and hung around so she wouldn't have to do anything else. After all, she thought, I came to the fair to ride the rides, not carry food all day. Mary Jo was very irritated and wanted B. J. to hurry up.

B. J. had problems of his own. He was helping Mr. Henry carry the tub of soda pop over to the picnic area. Mr. Henry was telling him to put his backbone into carrying the tub. Struggling to keep up with Mr. Henry's long steps, he was holding the tub handle with two hands.

Mr. Henry continued to say, "Come on, hean boy. I got to beat old man Slim at some checkers."

Dust was flying up as poor B. J. shuffled his feet. The soft dirt made it hard for him to keep in step with Mr. Henry's long strides. His hands and legs felt like they were on fire. It was a strain on him carrying the heavy tub.

B. J. was really trying to be brave. However, the weight from the tub was too much for the little boy. He thought, I'm not going to make it. I can feel the handle slipping out of my hands. How far is this picnic area? Determined not to act like a baby, B. J. continued to struggle.

Finally, Mr. Henry noticed the strain on his face and said, "Boy, yoes look like yoes tired. huh?"

B. J. said in a squeaky voice, "Yeah, sort of Mr. Henry."

"Well! Mr. Henry said in a deep baritone voice. "I'll go git one of de men folk to help. Now yoes just stay right heah and watch dem there sodie, hean boy."

"Wow!" B. J. burst out and said as he rubbed his red palms, "I need to get some feeling back in these hands. That is a job for two big men like Mr. Henry." He was so happy as he signed "whew!" He wiped the dust off his face and dusted the soft dirt off his sandals. He patiently waited for the men to return.

Old man Slim was hollering, "Come on, Henry, and take yoes medicine like a man cause yoes all readie beat!"

Mr. Slim continued to hound Mr. Henry as he approached the table where Mr. Henry was standing. "Yoes sees, Henry, the board is already fixed for yore whipping uh huh."

Mr. Henry was getting one of the men to help bring the tub back. "Yoes going to git the whipping of yoes life cause old Slim hean is the best." Slim kept talking.

"Go on old man and finish gitting the checkers set-up," Mr. Henry said. One of the men followed Mr. Henry back down to where B. J. was sitting. He was watching that tub of soda waters like a hound dog.

"Well youngin," Mr. Henry said, as they walked toward B. J. "Yoes can go on now. Us men can handle this tub now."

"Yes sir Mr. Henry and thanks," B. J. said as he ran off to find Mary Jo. The two men picked up the tub and walked over to the picnic area. Old man Slim was patiently waiting.

"Here I am.!" Mr. Henry said. "Now make your move, old man."

Mary Jo was over near the table talking to her mama when B. J. saw her. Immediately, he said, "Ain't you ready to go yet, Mary Jo? We ain't got all day, you know?" Mary Jo looking pitiful, said, "Mama, may I go now?"

"Yeah child!" Mrs. Finney said as she took out her "happy sack" and gave her two shiny quarters. "And make dat last yoes hean, young lady?" her mama said.

Anxious to go, Mary Jo kept saying, "Yes ma'am, yes ma'am, mama."
Mrs. Finney didn't lay the rule down this time and Mary Jo got away clean. They took off running across the picnic area. They quickly made their way to the fairway. She went to the Ferris wheel ticket booth first. She did not notice Billy Ray coming up the fairway.

However, B. J. spotted Billy Ray and immediately began to call his name. Looking at all of the attractions Billy Ray didn't see B. J. He had a big smile on his face as he eagerly waved his hands. He was trying to get Billy Ray's attention. This got Mary Jo's attention as she strained her eyes. She was trying hard to see what or whom B. J. was waving at. Coming up the fairway was Billy Ray.

Mary Jo turned around and noticed how good Billy Ray looked. He had on a striped red, white, and blue shirt that matched his white shorts and some brown cry baby sandals. She was so dumbfounded she stood speechless with her mouth open. She thought that this can't be the same boy we were with last month. Thinking hard, Mary Jo was trying to figure out where Billy Ray got the money to buy that outfit. Somebody must have given it to him. She had a big smile on her face.

I've had great fun traveling down memory lane with you. Stay with me on this sweet journey. I'll reveal Billy Ray's big secret in my next book, entitled, **"Hot Fun In The SummerTime!"**

www.ingramcontent.com/pod-product-compliance
Lightning Source LLC
Chambersburg PA
CBHW080607170426
43209CB00007B/1364